VIRTUALLY VEGAN

All-vegan recipes
with a non-vegan twist

VIRTUALLY VEGAN

HEATHER WHINNEY

NOURISH
EAT WELL, LIVE WELL

For my husband, Jos; my daughters, Kim and Lorna; my grandchildren, Max, Leo, Oscar and Annabelle; and my mum (Nanny).

First published in the UK and USA in 2018 by
Nourish, an imprint of Watkins Media Limited
19 Cecil Court
London WC2N 4EZ

enquiries@nourishbooks.com

Commissioning Editor: Kate Fox
Managing Editor: Daniel Hurst
Editor: Wendy Hobson
Designer: Glen Wilkins and Georgina Hewitt
Cover Design: Georgina Hewitt
Production: Uzma Taj
Commissioned photography: William Shaw
Food Stylist: Heather Whinney
Food Stylist Assistant: Jos Whinney
Prop Stylist: Lucy Harvey

A CIP record for this book is available from the British Library

ISBN: 978-1-84899-347-1

10 9 8 7 6 5 4 3 2 1

Typeset in Adobe Caslon Pro and News Gothic BT
Colour reproduction by XY Digital
Printed in China

Publisher's note
While every care has been taken in compiling the recipes for this book, Watkins Media Limited, or any other persons who have been involved in working on this publication, cannot accept responsibility for any errors or omissions, inadvertent or not, that may be found in the recipes or text, nor for any problems that may arise as a result of preparing one of these recipes. If you are pregnant or breastfeeding or have any special dietary requirements or medical conditions, it is advisable to consult a medical professional before following any of the recipes contained in this book.

Notes on the recipes
Unless otherwise stated:
Use medium fruit and vegetables
Use fresh herbs, spices and chillies
Do not mix metric, imperial and US cup measurements:
    1 tsp = 5ml 1 tbsp = 15ml 1 cup = 240ml

nourishbooks.com

Contents

Introduction

For many people, the expression 'virtually vegan' might seem like a contradiction. If you have fully adopted veganism, it's likely to be an ethical, or perhaps a nutritional, choice and implies a whole way of life.

But it's not often that people make a decision to become vegan overnight. It tends to be more evolution than revolution, as gradually their relationship with food changes in response to broad ethical issues or more personal health issues, for example. There are many thousands on the margins of that commitment; perhaps vegetarian, but also those who simply choose to cook meals free from animal products, dairy and eggs a few times a week. Sometimes this is intentional but, perhaps as often, it can be a happy accident. With increasing numbers of people wanting to cook in this way, it's never been more important to learn about the recipes and techniques that make the most of a plant-based diet.

I call myself a vegan 'dabbler'. I'm not a fully committed vegan, but I love cooking vegan food. It is a love affair that has lasted 30 years, from raising a family, cooking in vegetarian restaurants, and following a career as a food editor and recipe writer on national food and women's lifestyle magazines. So when a family member and a friend both announced recently that they were now almost vegan, it got me thinking about the type of food I cooked regularly at home. I realized it was, almost by accident, virtually vegan.

My favourite vegan recipes show just how interesting and enticing vegan food can be. I am confident this collection will be enjoyed by everyone, whether you are vegan, vegetarian, 'virtually vegan' or a full-on meat-eater who just enjoys some plant-based meals in your repertoire. Wherever vegans and non-vegans are sitting around the same table, sharing a meal, it provides the flexibility to offer the same dish tweaked in different ways, so nobody is left out. Whether your son or daughter is vegan, you're hosting a party with vegan and non-vegan guests, or if you're vegan yourself and looking for a dish to appeal to your omnivorous friends, these are tasty and appealing dishes that everyone can enjoy. And anyone who wants to learn more about great vegan cooking can make a start right here.

This book includes everything from brunches to desserts, from the simplest snacks to more impressive main courses, from nostalgic dishes to super-healthy choices. They dispel the myth that vegan food is bland –

delivering on flavour was my number one goal! And being a mum and a grandmother, I appreciate issues with time constraints and fussy eaters so recipes had to be easy on the shop, uncomplicated, with no hard-to-trace ingredients.

With any healthy diet, two key elements are variety and balance, and that applies to a vegan diet as much as to any other. The ways you can prepare and cook with vegetables, grains, pulses, nuts, fruit and seeds are countless, and I intend these recipes to show that vegan cooking is exciting. It's not about what you may have excluded from your diet but all about the gorgeous ingredients you can include. It is a thoughtful way of cooking – a big pan of a bubbling vegetable curry, a batch of piccalilli or a deliciously sweet marmalade cake can bring added joy knowing it has all been done without using any animal products. Plus there's the added bonus here that there are options for those who decide to stay 'virtually vegan' or not to take that route at all.

But do remember that veganism and full-on healthy don't necessarily go hand in hand. It is my belief that we all need chocolate cake in our lives – plus a few more sweet treats! My feeling is if you are going to eat cake or cookies just do it occasionally but make sure they are seriously good. Vegan baking does present a few challenges – for the obvious reason that you don't use eggs – but I have explained some new techniques and adapted some of my favourite recipes so they work beautifully without them. Sadly, though, the usual rules apply: just because they are vegan doesn't mean cakes are for every day, three times a day!

I wouldn't dream of trying to persuade you to become vegan. My aim is not to convert, but rather to gently introduce you to a selection of delicious and flexible vegan recipes that you'll enjoy – simple as that! In my experience, my bold and simple but gutsy recipes that put flavour first can win over the keenest meat-eater.

I am confident you will enjoy bringing this type of eating into your repertoire, with minimum effort. As a recipe writer, I want my food to be enjoyed, to be cooked on repeat, tweaked to add your own stamp and above all I want it to taste great – vegan or not!

The Virtually Vegan Storecupboard

Whether you are a committed vegan, or just dipping your toe into veganism, searching for expensive or difficult to find ingredients can be really offputting and take the joy out of cooking. Vegan-specific products like cheese substitutes are wonderful, but if a recipe relies on them, it can make it hard to get started. Throughout this book I have focused on familiar ingredients that can be found at your local shop or supermarket, and enjoyed by the whole family. I have noted a brand if it is one I particularly like and use regularly. You can add to your storecupboard while you shop, a few ingredients at a time, so you can make a meal with a minute's notice – just add your fruit and veg!

Milk alternatives

Coconut milk: Made from water and coconut milk, this has a distinctive flavour. A staple for the cupboard, it has numerous uses in sweet and savoury dishes and makes a good dairy replacement. Use the whole can by giving it a shake, or scoop off the creamy top when in need of a thicker cream or for whipping. Use it in ice creams, dips and sauces, soups, poaching vegetables or tofu, Thai curries, Indian curries, puddings and desserts, smoothies and cocktails!

Coconut drinking milk: Don't get this confused with the thicker, canned variety. It is rich and creamy with a higher fat content than some other dairy-free milks, but it can impart a particular flavour to your baking.

Oat milk: Made from soaked oats and water, this tastes just a little sweet with a slightly thicker texture. It is good for all cooking except gluten-free.

Soy milk: Made from water and soy beans, this is higher in protein than other dairy-free milks. It has a creamy texture and neutral flavour. It is stable at high temperatures and won't split when heated so it is good for all cooking and baking.

Unsweetened almond milk: Made from water and almonds, this is low in calories, good for all cooking, baking and delicious in lattes, but be aware that it may add a slight sweetness to your savoury dishes. You can also make your own.

Buttermilk: If a recipe calls for butter-milk, add a few drops of lemon juice to a non-dairy milk (soy milk works best because of its high protein) and leave it for 5 minutes.

Non-dairy spreads

There are a lot of spreads to choose from and it comes down to taste and texture preference. Substitute weight for weight for butter. Most margarines are now non-hydrogenated, but always read the label.

Olive oil spread: Made with olive oil and vegetable oil to give a light spread and often lower in calories than other options, this is good for shallow frying and spreading.

Soy spread: Often a cheaper option, use this for general cooking and shallow frying.

Sunflower spread: A light, creamy spread made from sunflower oil, this is great for pastry and cakes and all baking, including making buttercream.

Canned beans, pulses and vegetables

Beans and pulses are invaluable for the vegan storecupboard. Not only so you can whip up a chilli, curry, burgers or a salad but they are also power-packed nutritionally and provide vital protein and vitamins. They are super-convenient and have a long shelf life. I also use dried pulses (see page 12). But the other essential is a good can of tomatoes, which will always provide the base for a good meal.

Aduki beans: Use as a substitute for minced/ground meat, in pies and pasties, chillies and cottage pie.

Black-eyed beans: Great for Mexican and African-inspired dishes, you can also use them in rice and peas, stews, Tex Mex rice, empanadas, burritos and soups.

Borlotti beans: Use in chunky soups and casseroles.

Butter/lima beans: Use in salads, mash, bean cakes and fritters, tomato-based sauces and casseroles.

Cannellini beans: Use in pâtés and dips, Italian salads and soups.

Chickpeas/garbanzos: Perfect for hummus, salads, curries, channa masala, smashed on toast or for smoky Spanish dishes. The juice from the can, known as aquafaba, can be used as an egg replacement (see page 16).

Flageolet beans: Great for French-inspired dishes, cassoulets, salads and simmered with wine and herbs.

Haricot beans: Why not make your own baked beans?

Lentils: Brown, green and Puy lentils are available in cans and Puy lentils are available ready-cooked in pouches. They are good for adding protein and bulking out vegetable dishes such as stews and casseroles, and also ideal for salads, burgers, meatless balls, dahl, ragu and bakes.

Passata/sieved tomatoes: This is another definite must for the cupboard to use as a base for sauces, in curries, with rice, pasta or as a pizza topping. The best passata/sieved tomatoes I have found is an Italian brand called Valfrutta. I use their organic passata/sieved tomatoes as it is so good.

Pinto beans: Use for refried beans.

Plum tomatoes: If you have just one thing in the cupboard, make it this hero of the pantry. Use for sauces, casseroles, soups, pizza toppings, bakes, with rice, in Italian-based dishes, vegan moussaka, gumbos and curries.

Red kidney beans: Cook these in chillies, tacos, enchiladas, burgers and hot pots. Also nice added to salads.

Fridge and freezer food

Broad/fava beans: A few vegetables are just as good from frozen as fresh, and this is one of them. I always have a pack of broad/fava beans in the freezer. As well as tasting pretty good, they are a great protein choice so add lots to your dishes. To peel the skin away, once cooked, is down to choice; some recipes benefit from it and others don't. Broad/fava beans are great in Middle Eastern-style dishes but you can also use them in pâtés, salads, fritters, soups, stir-fries, with pasta, rice and as a bruschetta topping.

Garden peas: Don't treat these as just a side veg – they can be the star of the show and add a gorgeous sweetness to a dish. Use in risottos, fritters, soups, pastries, curries, pâtés and dips, salads, with pasta and in vegan pancakes.

Soy/edamame beans: Use in stir-fries, with rice, to accompany a vegan sushi, in salads, with tofu dishes, tossed with chilli and served with drinks.

Tempeh: Tempeh is fermented bean curd and consequently has a taste entirely different from tofu. It is also firmer in texture, making it perfect to roast or griddle in slices and great for stir-fries and chillies. It's high in protein, so good to eat as part of a vegan diet. You'll find it in health-food stores and the health-food aisle of major supermarkets.

Tofu – firm, silken and marinated: When cooked right, tofu is amazing as it has the ability to absorb any flavour and acts as a sponge (think red Thai curry – a tofu version, in my opinion, can knock spots off a meat one any day). It contains all the essential amino acids and protein, making it a perfect choice for vegans. It is also known as bean curd and is derived from the soy bean. Keep a selection in the fridge. Use firm tofu for stir-frying, curries or bakes and silken for desserts, shakes and dressings. You can also freeze it.

Dried food

Agar agar: This is derived from a sea vegetable and is a vegan alternative to gelatine. It is neutral in taste so you can use it to thicken anything from jellies to mousses.

Beans and pulses: I like to have canned pulses for convenience (see page 10) but when I have a little more time or I've planned ahead, I use dried. They are cheaper and in some instances taste better. You do, however, have to pre-soak some, then cook some for a couple of hours. Don't over-buy unless you know you will use them. Teamed with grains, they will supply all your amino-acid needs. My storecupboard favourites are: black-eyed, black turtle, borlotti, butter/lima, cannellini, chickpeas/garbanzos (dried make the best hummus), haricot, kidney and pinto.

Bouillon powder: A good stock is invaluable in all cooking, but especially in vegan cooking, where there is no meat base to provide the flavour. I use Marigold vegan stock as it is flavoursome without being overpowering and it is lower in salt than some other varieties.

Chocolate, dark: It's good to know you can eat chocolate on a vegan diet! Have some Lindt Excellence (70%, 85% or 90% cocoa solids) in the cupboard so you can whip up a cake or just enjoy a square for a snack. There's lots of specific vegan dark chocolate brands but this just happens to be vegan.

Cocoa powder, 100% cocoa powder: Yes, you can have hot chocolate if you are vegan and a pretty tasty one at that. Green & Black is my favourite brand, but look for any that is 100% cocoa powder (with no added milk) and use it for drinks and in baking.

Cornflour/cornstarch: Use as a thickener for sauces and home-made custard.

Custard powder: Go ahead and make your own if you wish (as for Peach & Raspberry Whisky Trifle on page 196) but nothing beats a jug of hot custard over your fruit crumble made with Bird's custard powder (I prefer this brand and the kids will too). This is one of those accidental vegan products and it sits proudly in my cupboard!

Fruits: Keep a varied selection of dried fruits in stock and add them to both sweet and savoury dishes. Think dried apricots to sweeten up a curry or dried figs in a pilaf. They add texture and a new flavour dimension. They don't spoil very quickly so you can stock up on them, although remember they are high in sugars and calories, so keep the portions low. My favourites are: apricots, sour cherries, cranberries, dates, figs, prunes, raisins and sultanas/golden raisins.

Grains: Where would we be without grains? Wholegrains are an essential part of the vegan diet, providing fibre, protein and more. They are super-easy to cook with, bulk out dishes and fill us up. Use in salads, stir-fries,

pilafs and in baking. My storecupboard favourites are: bulgur wheat, couscous, farro, freekeh, pearl barley and quinoa.

Lentils: Brown, green, Puy, red and yellow, dried lentils are a great standby that provide vegetable protein. They all cook up relatively quick and make a thrifty meal, so use them in curries, burgers, dahls, salads and stews.

Nuts: An extraordinary plant food that introduce protein and omega-3 into your diet, nuts are ideal for snacking on (about a handful a day) and cooking with. Toss into salads, add to rice dishes, grind for nut butters, use as a topping and, of course, for desserts and baking. My storecupboard favourites are: whole, flaked and ground almonds, cashews, hazelnuts, macadamia, dry roasted peanuts, pecans, pine nuts, pistachios and walnuts.

Noodles: Vegans should look for egg-free noodles – normally vermicelli, flat or rice noodles, and some soba (check the pack).

Pasta: Like noodles, choose egg-free dried pasta but check the pack. Fresh pasta is usually made with egg, unless you make your own (see page 110).

Polenta/cornmeal: I had a love/hate relationship with polenta/cornmeal eaten as a savoury dish until I ate in in the mountains in Italy topped with wild mushrooms – delicious! Polenta/cornmeal chips/fries are also pretty good. I haven't included polenta/

cornmeal in any recipes but I think it is good to have in the cupboard, as it is very useful in cakes. You can buy it as a meal, or pre-cooked, ready to slice and griddle.

Porcini mushrooms: A small quantity adds bags of flavour. Soak before using, then run the soaking water through a fine-mesh sieve/strainer, as it can be gritty, and use that too. These mushrooms will add a real gutsy, 'meaty' flavour to your stews and chillies.

Rice: Keep a good selection – brown, white basmati, wild, red – to make a meal from them, stir up a risotto or a pilaf, or as an accompaniment.

Sea vegetables: I always have nori and wakame in stock as I like to add it to my miso soups, rice or ramen dishes. It provides vital nutrition, including vitamin B, magnesium and zinc.

Seeds: These pack a rich nutritional content, so get munching! Toast in a dry frying pan and sprinkle over food, add to smoothies, granolas or stir into rice dishes. My storecupboard favourites are: flax/linseed, poppy, pumpkin, black and white sesame, and sunflower.

Jars and sauces

Artichoke hearts: I love fresh artichokes, but a jar of grilled artichokes in oil is a good cupboard standby and fabulous to toss into salads and bakes.

Chilli sauces and pastes: These seem to grow and accumulate in my cupboard but good staples to start with are sriracha, piri piri and sambal oelek. Sometimes a drizzle or spoonful of chilli is just what a dish is begging for! For chilli paste, I buy a Korean one called Hot Pepper Paste, or use Korean red pepper powder (*gochugaru*).

Gherkins and cornichons: These make an appearance in my food quite often as they add the piquancy that is so often needed. Slice, chop and stir into your rice dishes, salads or even hot pots.

Harissa paste: To add richness and depth – oh, and heat! – harissa is great stirred into North African-inspired dishes but also good with roasted veggies or in a sauce or soup. My favourite branded product is Belazu Rose Harissa.

Maple syrup: This is expensive, but there are different grades. It is very sweet so use sparingly. It is one of my favourite sweetener choices for cakes, desserts and savoury dishes as honey is a no-no for vegan cooking.

Marmite/yeast extract: This is non-negotiable for the storecupboard even if you don't enjoy it slathered on toast. It adds so much flavour to stews, chillies and pie fillings, giving them the umami hit that is sometimes needed, so buy a big jar!

Miso: I always have a white and a red miso paste in the refrigerator (bought in tubs from the supermarket or Asian store) because they have completely different flavour profiles. The white is soy beans fermented with rice. It is light and sweet and you use it in soups, dressings, sauces and glazes. The red is soy beans fermented with barley or other grains. It has a depth and richness to it that adds a real umami kick to your food. Use it in soups and stews.

Mustards: Don't be shy with mustard when you are cooking without meat and fish. For flavour, you have to be more imaginative and mustard really cuts it by adding some tang. Stir it into pie fillings, chillies, soups, casseroles and dressings. My storecupboard favourites are: English, Dijon and wholegrain.

Nut butters: Choose a sugar-free one and stir it into sweet or savoury dishes. It will add bags of oomph to a vegetable casserole, is good for your baking, from cookies to cakes and, of course, to spread on toast. My storecupboard favourites are: almond, cashew and peanut.

Oils: I tend to cook with an average-priced extra virgin olive oil and have a couple of good ones – one fruity and one grassy – for drizzling and dressings. Use all oils in baking and cooking. My storecupboard favourites are: coconut, nut oils, olive oil, extra virgin olive oil, rapeseed and sunflower.

Olives, green and black: These are perfect to toss into a sauce, roast, salad, or to serve

with pasta or pizza or blitz for a dip, dressing or pâté.

Pesto: Pesto is not just for pasta! I stir it into many sauces and tomato-based dishes, bubbling on the hob, or stir it into dressings. My favourite brand is Sacla, which does a gluten-free and a dairy-free version.

Preserved lemons: For a tart and lemony flavour, slice and stir the skin into North African dishes or add some zing to rice and grains. It has the ability to transform a regular dish into something special.

Soy sauce: Again another umami ingredient, and a definite for Asian foods, stir-fries and dressings. Keep dark and light in the cupboard; the dark is saltier.

Sun-dried tomatoes: These need reconstituting in warm water if bought dried, otherwise buy in oil. Intensely flavoured, you can chop them into one-pots, dressings, salads, tarts and muffins.

Tahini: This roasted sesame seed paste has a taste like no other and nothing else can really be substituted for it (other than roasted and ground white sesame seeds). It gives dishes a wonderfully distinct, slightly bitter flavour. Use it in sauces, dips and dressings and to add an earthy edge to casseroles.

Thai curry pastes, red and green: Stir into sauces, curries, soups or dressings, or toss with veggies or potatoes for a spicy roast. I

like the Blue Dragon brand. Note that some brands may contain shrimp paste.

Tomato purée/paste: Sauté it at the beginning of cooking with onion and garlic to add masses of depth to sauces and casseroles. It is intense; a small squirt adds a powerful flavour boost.

Vinegars: A splash of acidic flavour adds a real zing to food – I frequently use vinegar instead of wine to deglaze a pan after cooking. My storecupboard favourites are: apple cider, balsamic, cider, white wine, raspberry, red wine, rice.

Wasabi: A little goes a long way as it is hot! Use sparingly in dressings, rice and one-pots.

Herbs and spices

Every cook needs a good spice rack. My favourites are: cayenne pepper, dried chilli flakes, Chinese five-spice, ground cinnamon, ground cumin, garam masala, whole nutmeg, oregano, paprika, sumac, ground turmeric and za'atar.

Wine

Animal-derived ingredients are used in the processing of some wines, and if you want a recipe that calls for wine to be vegan then it's important to check this. Manufacturers are getting better at putting this information on the label, but if in doubt then look out for an ingredients list including albumen, casein, gelatine or isinglass, which are all non-vegan.

The Art of Vegan Baking

Baking is a science – or so we are always told – but I think that makes the whole thing seem rather intimidating. I think baking is fun and exciting, and a good excuse to show off! But it's true that vegan baking presents a few challenges, as most standard recipes rely on some form of dairy.

So here are a few tips to ensure your vegan baking creates fabulous results. The recipes in the Desserts and Sweet Treats chapters are pretty straightforward – nothing too tricky or time-consuming – but you can use the conversions here for any baking recipe you like. Just experiment!

These recipes don't require any special equipment, but it's handy to have a few tools of the trade to make life a bit simpler: a hand-held electric whisk or food mixer; various good-quality cake and bake tins (cheap ones tend to buckle over time); measuring cups or scales; and a reliable oven. These will all ensure you get the best results.

Eggs

Baking usually relies on eggs for both binding and rising; as a cake bakes, eggs add volume and structure in the form of protein and also add moisture to the bake and help ingredients to emulsify and hold together. When eggs are beaten they act as a leavening agent and add air into a batter, which will then expand and make your cake rise.

How do I bake without eggs?

Don't expect exactly the same results when baking without eggs, then you won't be disappointed. It can be trial and error at first,

but as long as your cake is tasty and moist that is the main thing.

Eggs are one of the highest food allergens so even if you're not vegan, baking without eggs can be a useful skill when baking for friends.

Any substance that can replicate the properties of an egg can be used in baking.

Aquafaba: This is the juice from a can of chickpeas/garbanzos, or if you boil your own beans from dried, you can also use this water. Proteins travel from the beans into the water, which can then be used as the ideal egg replacement. Depending on what you are using it for, you may wish to heat it so it reduces more to the consistency of egg white or you can whisk it to make a fluffy and light mixture to use in meringues. Generally 3 tablespoons of aquafaba is equivalent to 1 egg. Multiply up as needed. You can freeze aquafaba for up to a month so get into the habit of freezing the juice whenever you cook chickpeas/garbanzos.

Chia seeds: Another good swap for eggs is chia seeds mixed with water until they reach a gelatinous consistency, which then works as a binding agent rather like eggs. A mixture of 1 tablespoon of chia seeds to 3 tablespoons of water is equivalent to 1 egg. Multiply up as needed.

Flax seeds: You can also use flax seeds exactly the same way but they have a stronger flavour than chia seeds.

Butter

Butter in baking helps make a cake tender, light and moist. It also adds flavour. It gives a delicious 'crumb' to pastry, cookies and cakes.

How do I bake without butter?

Substituting butter is easy as you can use like-for-like weight of a vegan spread or margarine, or solid coconut oil, if you prefer (although I think this has too much flavour). Obviously the flavour of your choice of spread is important as it will impact on the overall flavour of your baking. I use Biona organic sunflower spread as I think it is creamy enough for cakes, tasty enough for cookies and shortbread and it makes really 'short' light pastry. Plus it is good enough to be enjoyed by the whole family.

It does, however, contain palm oil, which is an ingredient many people wish to avoid. It is not something I would use to spread on toast, for example, and I don't bake regularly enough for it to be a worry, but it works so well in cakes, pastry and buttercream.

Margarine is not dairy-based, although some can contain trace amounts of animal products. Read the label and avoid any with whey, lactose, casein or caseinates. Watch out, too, for the source of the vitamin D. It can come from plant sources and therefore be suitable or it can come from lanolin (washed lamb's wool) and therefore not.

Some vegetable-based margarines may be accidently vegan.

Look for ones that contains no palm oil if this is a concern for you.

Milk

Milk adds flavour, richness and helps with the texture of baked goods.

How do I bake without milk?

As with butter, milk is easy to substitute with a non-dairy milk and be used like-for-like in baking as it has the same consistency as milk. There are plenty to choose from and we all have our favourites, but do choose one that is unsweetened. It can impart a flavour into your baking depending on what you choose.

Cream

Cream adds fat, richness, creaminess and thickness to baking.

How do I bake without cream?

Double/heavy cream: For thick cream, use canned coconut milk. It can be used for whipping by allowing the milk to separate in the can (putting it in the refrigerator can speed this up), then scooping away the top creamy layer and whisking vigorously. Use this for serving and for toppings in baking. Or you can mix it with a dairy-free milk to lighten it up or use for pouring.

Single/light cream: For a lower-fat substitute for cream, whisk silken tofu until smooth. This is also good to use as a thickener in baking.

Yogurt: Whip soy yogurt with dairy-free milk for a creamy accompaniment to sweet pastries and cakes.

Gelling agents

Gelatine is used in ordinary baking as a thickener and setting agent.

How do I bake without gelatine ?

Agar is a naturally derived gelatine which comes from sea vegetables. It is unflavoured and easy to use for anything you need thickening or setting. It is actually more powerful than gelatine and will set quicker. It can be used in any recipe that calls for gelatine. A teaspoon of powdered agar is the equivalent to 8 teaspoons of gelatine. Like gelatine, you must dissolve it in water first before heating it. As a rule of thumb, you need 1 teaspoon of agar to set 240ml/ 8fl oz/1 cup of water.

Flour

You can obviously use all flours as the baking recipes aren't aimed at being gluten-free. With vegan baking, it is important to increase the 'rise' in a cake. Apple cider vinegar is often added to vegan recipes for its leavening qualities. The acids in the vinegar helps to activate flour, baking powder or bicarbonate of soda/baking soda, which enhances the leavening or rising of your baking and results in a better crumb. You won't be able to taste a few drops in baking.

Baking tips

Baking without dairy and eggs is a whole new way of making cakes, cookies and desserts, and as with any kind of baking, it takes time and patience to get it right. You will get to know which products or ingredients you prefer to use and which get the best results.

- Read the recipe through from start to finish first.
- Weigh out all the ingredients first and keep to the same measurement system throughout, don't switch.
- Preheat the oven before you start so it is at temperature when your creation is ready to bake.
- Don't open the oven door early on in the baking.
- Sift all flours, baking powders, cocoa, icing sugars, and so on.
- Get the cake mixture into the oven as soon as it is ready.

- Always make sure to use the specified cake pan sizes.
- If you are creaming a cake mixture, get as much air into it as you can and don't overwork when adding the flour otherwise you will lose all that precious air.
- Use measuring spoons for accuracy and level them off with a knife.

Cake troubleshooting

Cake sank in the middle: The batter was probably too thin, you did not include enough baking powder or perhaps you had too much sugar or fat.

Cake didn't rise: The batter was too thin so reduce the amount of liquid. Or it could be that there was not enough baking powder.

Cake was dry: This usually means it has been overbaked or not enough liquid or fat was added to the mix.

1

BREAKFASTS
& BRUNCHES

Raspberry & chocolate granola

If you prepare your own granola, you have complete control over what goes into it – which is a rather nice thought and means you can feel quite virtuous when are eating your breakfast. This recipe is almost super-healthy – I just couldn't resist the addition of a little chocolate – but you can leave the cocoa out if it is too much in the morning. A granola should be crunchy, slightly chewy and not too sweet, so you get different textures in each mouthful. This makes a large jarful and will keep well for a couple of weeks.

Makes a 700g/1lb 9oz jar
Prep: 15 mins Cook: 25 mins

2 tbsp sunflower spread
3–4 tbsp maple syrup
300g/10½oz/3 cups rolled oats
1 large handful of pumpkin seeds
about 250g/9oz/2 cups mixed nuts,
    such as almonds, hazelnuts and
    pecans, roughly chopped
1 tbsp cocoa/unsweetened chocolate
    powder, at least 70% cocoa
100g/3½oz/¾ cup dried fruit, such
    as raisins, cranberries, sour
    cherries and apricots, roughly
    chopped

TO SERVE
almond milk
1 handful of fresh raspberries

1 Preheat the oven to 190°C/375°F/Gas 5 and line a large baking/cookie sheet with parchment paper.

2 Put the sunflower spread and maple syrup in a pan and heat gently until melted. Put the oats, pumpkin seeds, nuts and cocoa/unsweetened chocolate powder in a large bowl and mix together well. Pour in the melted maple syrup mixture and stir to combine.

3 Spread the mixture out onto the prepared baking/cookie sheet and bake for about 20–25 minutes, or until golden. Give it a stir every now and then. Leave to cool, then stir in the dried fruit. Store in an airtight jar until ready to eat.

4 Serve with a little almond milk and topped with fresh raspberries – or it's nice with banana too!

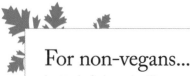

For non-vegans...
Instead of almond milk,
this granola is delicious
with a dollop of crème fraîche
or yogurt.

Pancakes with cherries & maple syrup

These are sweet and beautifully light and fluffy. They take a little longer to cook than regular pancakes but the exact time depends on how thick you make them – a small ladle is a good measure. You can make these free form or pour the mixture into a circular metal cutter in the pan for a perfect round.

Makes about 10 x 12cm/4½in
  pancakes
Prep: 15 mins Cook: 30 mins

150g/5oz/1¼ cups plain/all-purpose
  flour, sifted
2 tsp baking powder, sifted
2 tbsp golden caster/superfine sugar
a pinch of salt
1 tbsp rapeseed oil
grated zest of 1 lemon
sunflower spread, for cooking

FOR THE TOPPING
about 400g/14oz/2½ cups pitted
  black cherries
about ½–1 tbsp demerara/turbinado
  sugar

TO SERVE
juice of 1 lemon
a drizzle of maple syrup

1 Put the flour and baking powder in a bowl, then stir in the sugar and salt. Mix the oil with 300ml/10½fl oz/scant 1¼ cups of cold water, then gradually pour it into the flour, stirring continuously. Use a balloon whisk to get rid of any lumps, then stir in the lemon zest. Leave to one side.

2 Put the cherries in a pan, trickle in a little water and add sugar to taste – use less if the cherries are sweet. Turn to coat the cherries, then simmer gently for about 10 minutes until the cherries just begin to start bursting. Remove from the heat and leave to one side.

3 To make the pancakes, add a tablespoon of sunflower spread to a crêpe pan or non-stick frying pan over a medium heat, then spoon in about a tablespoon of the batter. Turn the heat to high and let it cook undisturbed for 1–1½ minutes until bubbles start to appear on the top and the underside is starting to turn pale golden. Use a palette knife/metal spatula and begin to loosen around the edges and underneath. If it moves quite freely, it is ready to flip over, although you may need to use a fish slice to do this. Now cook the other side for about 1 minute until pale golden, then slide the pancake out of the pan and keep it warm. Continue cooking the pancakes, using more sunflower spread as needed, until you have used all the mixture.

4 Layer the pancakes with the cherries, top with a squeeze of lemon juice and a drizzle of maple syrup and dig in.

Tempeh roast traybake breakfast

Letting the oven do all the work is just what is needed for a weekend breakfast. Tempeh is packed with umami flavours so it hits the spot in the morning, especially with the sweetness of the cherry tomatoes and peppers to cut through the richness. A squirt of sriracha hot chilli sauce is pretty good with this.

Serves 4
Prep: 10 mins Cook: 30 mins

400g/14oz/3⅓ cups cubed tempeh
1 tbsp olive oil
1 tbsp tamari soy sauce
about 3 medium potatoes, peeled
    and diced into 2cm/¾in pieces
2–3 red peppers, halved, deseeded
    and roughly chopped
400g/14oz cherry tomatoes
2 avocados, pitted and roughly
    chopped, then tossed in a
    squeeze of lemon juice
sea salt and freshly ground black
    pepper
warm crusty bread or toast, to serve

1 Preheat the oven to 200°C/400°F/Gas 6.

2 Put the tempeh in a large roasting pan, drizzle with half the oil and a splash of the tamari and toss together. Add the potatoes and peppers, toss with remaining oil and season with salt and pepper. Roast for about 15 minutes.

3 Add the tomatoes and cook for a further 5–15 minutes, or until everything is tender and crisp. Transfer to a serving dish, gently stir in the avocado and take it straight to the table so everyone can tuck in and enjoy with warm crusty bread or toast.

For non-vegans...
Cook a few sausages in another roasting pan in the oven for about 30 minutes, or until nicely browned and cooked through, then serve alongside the traybake.

Vietnamese pancakes with mushrooms

These are savoury crêpes that are eaten in Vietnam and don't use an egg for the batter. The first one you make is tricky and will probably end up in the bin, but persevere and they will get easier. I've kept the filling simple – it is breakfast time, after all! – but add more ingredients to your taste. They've never tasted quite as good as when I enjoyed them on holiday in Vietnam but the flavours certainly hit the spot.

Serves 4
Prep: 15 mins Cook: 20 mins

200g/7oz/1⅓ cups rice flour, sifted
1 tbsp cornflour/cornstarch, sifted
1 tsp ground turmeric
400ml/14fl oz can of
    coconut milk
1 large handful of beansprouts
1 handful of coriander/cilantro
    leaves, chopped
a little vegetable oil, for frying

FOR THE MUSHROOMS
a drizzle of sesame oil
about 400g/14oz button
    mushrooms, finely sliced
1 tbsp rice vinegar
a pinch of demerara/turbinado sugar
juice of ½ lime
sea salt and freshly ground black
    pepper

1 Put the rice flour, cornflour/cornstarch and turmeric in a bowl and mix. Season well with salt and pepper, then stir in the coconut milk, whisking as you go, followed by 300ml/10½fl oz/scant 1¼ cups of cold water. Whisk until thoroughly blended and there are no lumps. Put the batter to one side while you cook the mushrooms.

2 Heat the sesame oil in a frying pan, add the mushrooms and cook on a high heat for a couple of minutes until the mushrooms start to release their liquid. Mix the vinegar, demerara/turbinado sugar and lime juice together and season with salt and pepper. Pour it over the mushrooms and stir to coat.

3 Heat a tiny amount of oil in a non-stick frying pan until hot, then add a ladleful of batter – you'll be making about 8 pancakes. Leave it undisturbed for a couple of minutes, or until the bottom begins to crisp. Spoon in some mushrooms and cook for a minute or so more, or until the base is golden and comes away easily from the pan. Add some beansprouts and coriander/cilantro, fold the pancake over and remove from the pan using a fish slice. Serve straight away. Then continue making the next one.

For non-vegans...
Add a handful of cooked prawns/shrimp or chopped cooked chicken to the pancake, fold and serve.

Egyptian-style broad beans with tahini sauce

I am savoury all the way for breakfast, and this is nice to serve as something a little different for a weekend brunch. I've used frozen broad/fava beans which, although not so authentic, are much quicker than using dried, but you can use fresh if they are in season. The tahini sauce can be thinned down by adding more water if you prefer a drizzle. Dukkah is a nutty spice often made with a mixture of toasted hazelnuts, sesame seeds, ground coriander and salt. Serve this with flatbreads, as there is plenty of delicious mopping up to do!

Serves 4
Prep: 15 mins Cook: 40 mins

400g/14oz/2⅔ cups frozen broad/
   fava beans, defrosted
1 tbsp olive oil
1 onion, finely chopped
2 garlic cloves, finely chopped
1 tsp ground cumin
3 tomatoes, finely chopped
1 handful of flatleaf parsley leaves,
   finely chopped
a large pinch of dukkah spice mix
   (optional)
sea salt and freshly ground black
   pepper

FOR THE TAHINI SAUCE
1 garlic clove, crushed
100g/3½oz/½ cup tahini
juice of ½–1 lemon

TO SERVE
3 tomatoes, halved and diced
flatbreads
lemon wedges

1 You can cook the beans in hot water for 3–4 minutes, then drain and peel, if you wish, or you can add them straight to the pot.

2 Heat the oil in a large, shallow, heavy-based pan. Add the onion, season with salt and pepper and cook over a medium heat for 2–3 minutes until beginning to soften. Stir in the garlic and cumin and cook for a few seconds more, then add the broad/fava beans and stir well so they are coated in the onion mixture. Add the tomatoes and turn gently to coat, then pour in 400ml/14fl oz/1⅔ cups hot water from the kettle. Bring to the boil, then reduce to a simmer and cook gently, stirring occasionally, for about 30–40 minutes, crushing and mashing the beans with the edge of a wooden spoon. Stir in most of the parsley. Top up with more hot water from the kettle as it cooks, if needed. Taste and season some more if needed. Remove from the heat and leave to one side.

3 While the beans are cooking, mix together the garlic, tahini, lemon juice and 100ml/3½fl oz/scant ½ cup water and season to taste with a little salt. You need to taste and keep adjusting, adding a little more lemon juice or salt until it is just right. Serve the broad/fava beans with a large spoonful of tahini sauce and sprinkled with the dukkah, if using, and parsley. Serve with tomatoes, flatbreads and lemon wedges on the side.

For non-vegans...
You could top the dish with a
soft-boiled egg.

Vegan sausages with baked beans

Make these the day before you want to serve them as the sauce needs quite a long simmer and the sausages are best left chilling in the refrigerator overnight. The sausages bring an umami flavour – filled with Marmite and mushrooms – so they taste incredibly savoury and rich and hold together because of the stewed apple and breadcrumbs. They may not win the best-looking sausage in class but they are super-tasty and that's what counts.

Serves 4 (makes 8 sausages)
Prep: 20 mins Cook: 1½ hours,
   plus resting overnight if possible

1 tbsp olive oil
1 red onion, finely chopped
2 garlic cloves, finely chopped
1 tsp paprika
1 tbsp red wine vinegar
1 tbsp dark brown sugar
400g/14oz can of tomatoes
2 x 400g/14oz cans of cannellini
   beans, drained and rinsed
sea salt and freshly ground black
   pepper

FOR THE SAUSAGES

2 eating/dessert apples, peeled,
   cored and roughly chopped
1 tbsp olive oil, plus extra for frying
1 onion, finely chopped
2 garlic cloves, finely chopped

continued opposite

For non-vegans...
Add 200g/7oz of chopped bacon after the onions and cook until golden, or serve the beans with pork sausages.

1 First make the beans. Heat the oil in a large, heavy-based pan. Add the onion, season with salt and pepper and cook over a medium heat for 2–3 minutes until the onion is beginning to soften. Stir in the garlic and paprika and cook for a few seconds more, then add the vinegar and sugar and stir until it dissolves. Snip the tomatoes in the can to break them up, then add them to the pan and break them further with a wooden spoon against the side of the pan. Fill up the empty can with hot water from the kettle (be careful as the can will be hot) and add to the pan. Tip in the cannellini beans, bring to the boil, then turn the heat down and simmer with the lid partially on for about 1 hour, or until thickened, checking and stirring occasionally.

2 While the beans are cooking, make the sausages. Put the apples in a small saucepan, trickle in a little water and cook over a low heat for about 5 minutes until soft, then mash with a fork and leave to one side.

3 Heat the oil in a frying pan. Add the onion, season with salt and pepper and cook for 2–3 minutes until beginning to soften. Stir in the garlic, sage and rosemary and cook for a few seconds more. Add the mushrooms and cook for about 5–6 minutes, breaking them up with the edge of a wooden spoon as they cook. Stir in the Marmite and mustard, then add the stewed apple and breadcrumbs and stir until really well combined. Season to taste with salt and pepper, if needed, although it will be quite salty from the Marmite. Leave to cool, transfer to a bowl then put in the refrigerator to chill.

2 sage leaves, finely chopped

a few rosemary stalks, leaves finely chopped

400g/14oz chestnut/cremini mushrooms, finely chopped in a food processor if you have one

2 tsp Marmite

1 tsp Dijon mustard

100g/3½oz/1⅔ cups fine fresh breadcrumbs

1 handful of flour, for dusting

olive oil, for frying

4 Remove the mixture from the refrigerator and with floured hands scoop up 8 equal-size balls, depending on how big you want your sausages to be – you can make more small ones if you prefer. Roll into balls, then shape into sausages, sit them on a baking sheet and put in the refrigerator to firm up for 20 minutes or leave overnight (the beans will be also good made the day before and reheated).

5 When ready to cook the sausages, heat a little oil in a non-stick frying pan and add a few sausages at a time. Cook for about 4–5 minutes, or until golden on one side, then turn and cook until golden on all sides and cooked through.

6 Reheat the beans, topping up with a little hot water from the kettle if needed. Add the sausages to the pan, being careful they don't break up, and serve when piping hot.

Slow roasted tomatoes & sumac on sourdough

At the weekend you can come downstairs, put your tomatoes in the oven and let them do their thing – roasting them really coaxes the flavour out. Cook plenty of tomatoes in one batch, then keep them in the refrigerator to reheat for another day.

Serves 2
Prep: 5 mins Cook: 1 hour

about 8–10 tomatoes, halved horizontally

1–2 tsp sumac

a drizzle of olive oil

sea salt and freshly ground black pepper

slices of sourdough bread, to serve

1 Preheat the oven to 160°C/325°F/Gas 3.

2 Put the tomatoes cut-side up in a roasting pan, sprinkle over the sumac, drizzle with olive oil and season well with salt and pepper. Roast for 1 hour until lightly coloured and wrinkled.

3 When almost ready, toast the sourdough bread. Spoon the tomatoes on top and squash them into the toast with the back of your fork. Season with more pepper, if needed, and serve.

For non-vegans...
You could add some crisply grilled bacon.

Tofu vegeree

This makes a great brunch, especially if you have had a few wines the night before! It's all about the spices – if you get those right you've cracked it. I think a bit of heat is essential but it's your choice. I've used brown rice as this is my preference for its nuttiness – if you prefer fluffy white rice, it will be just as good. And if you have any leftover rice, it's a great way to use it up. Either way, you will need to reduce the cooking time slightly.

Serves 4
Prep: 30 mins Cook: 40 mins

310g/11oz/1¾ cups brown basmati
    rice
2 sweet potatoes, peeled and diced
1 tbsp olive oil
1½ tbsp dairy-free spread
1 onion, finely chopped
2 garlic cloves, finely chopped
1 green chilli, deseeded and finely
    chopped
2 tsp garam masala
1 tsp turmeric
1 tsp coriander seeds, crushed
160g/5¾oz pack of marinated tofu
    pieces
100g/3½oz/¾cup frozen peas,
    defrosted
sea salt and freshly ground black
    pepper

TO SERVE
1 handful of coriander/cilantro
    leaves
2 spring onions/scallions, trimmed
    and finely chopped
1 lemon, cut into wedges

1 Put the rice in a pan, add twice as much water and a pinch of salt and bring to the boil. Turn the heat down and simmer with the lid on for about 25–30 minutes, or until tender and the water has been absorbed. Leave to one side with the lid on.

2 Meanwhile, put the sweet potato in a pan of salted water, bring to the boil, then turn the heat down and simmer for 5–6 minutes, or until the sweet potato is tender but still has a bite. Drain well and leave to one side.

3 Heat the oil and dairy-free spread in a large, deep frying pan, add the onion and cook for 2–3 minutes until soft. Stir in the garlic, season with salt and pepper and cook for a minute more. Stir in the green chilli, garam masala, turmeric and coriander seeds and cook for 1–2 minutes. Carefully stir in the cooked sweet potato, tofu pieces and peas and cook for a couple of minutes.

4 Tip in the rice and stir really well so every grain is coated in the sauce. Season to taste with salt and pepper. Sprinkle over the coriander/cilantro leaves and spring onions/scallions and serve with lemon wedges.

For non-vegans...
Add a little flaked smoked fish to the pan at the same time as you tip in the rice. Allow it to warm through before serving.

Breakfast scramble with spinach, chilli & tomatoes

This is not just for breakfast time and would also make a great lunchtime dish or a quick supper for one or two. Silken tofu scrambles perfectly, and it takes on the flavours of the spices and vegetables so well. It makes a good storecupboard standby.

Serves 4
Prep: 5 mins Cook: 15 mins

1 tbsp olive oil
1½ tbsp sunflower spread
3 spring onions/scallions, trimmed
    and finely chopped
1 green chilli, deseeded and finely
    chopped
a pinch of ground turmeric
a pinch of sumac
340g/11¾oz/2⅔ cups of silken tofu
300g/10½oz spinach leaves
4 tomatoes, halved, deseeded and
    finely chopped
1 handful of coriander/cilantro
    leaves, chopped
sea salt and freshly ground black
    pepper

TO SERVE
soy yogurt with almond (optional)
lemon wedges

1 Heat the oil and sunflower spread in a large, non-stick frying pan. Add the onions, season with salt and pepper and cook for a couple of minutes until the onions begin to soften.

2 Stir in the chilli, turmeric and sumac and cook for a few seconds, then add the silken tofu, crush it with a fork, stirring to combine all the flavours, and cook for about 5 minutes. Add the spinach leaves and keep stirring for a minute or so until they wilt.

3 Stir in the tomatoes and half the coriander/cilantro, taste and season some more if needed. Garnish with the remaining coriander/cilantro and serve with a dollop of yogurt and a lemon wedge on the side.

For non-vegans...
Dairy yogurt and scrambled eggs would work just as well in this dish.

Vegetable pho

Pho is eaten for breakfast all over Vietnam. It is usually made with beef broth so this isn't truly authentic, but is a simplified version of a recipe I was taught at a cookery school in Vietnam. It's a real treat to have a fresh-tasting, fragrant and cleansing soup for breakfast. I'm not suggesting you rustle this up midweek before racing off to work, of course. It is more of a leisurely weekend brunch. It is filling and low in fat and I love the way it keeps you going and stops you getting hungry again before lunch!

Serves 4
Prep: 10 mins Cook: 40 mins

4 cloves
4 star anise
2 cinnamon sticks
3 cardamom pods, bruised
a pinch of sea salt
a few black peppercorns
3 tbsp light soy sauce
5cm/1¾in piece of fresh root ginger
20g/1oz dried shiitake mushrooms
a pinch of vegetable stock powder
2 pak choy/bok choy, trimmed and
    leaves separated
1 handful of spinach leaves
a pinch of chilli flakes (optional)
4 bundles rice noodles, soaked in
    hot water as per pack instruction,
    then drained
1 large handful of beansprouts

1 Preheat the oven to 190°C/375°F/Gas 5.

2 Put the cloves, star anise, cinnamon sticks and cardamom pods in a small roasting pan and cook in the oven for 15 minutes until fragrant.

3 Fill a pan with water, add a pinch of salt and the black peppercorns, then add the roasted spices, soy sauce, ginger and dried mushrooms, bring to the boil, then turn down the heat and simmer for 20 minutes.

4 Strain into a clean pan, season with a little vegetable stock and add a pinch of salt. Bring to the boil, then reduce to a simmer. Add the pak choy/bok choy, spinach and chilli flakes, if using, and cook for 5 minutes until the vegetables are wilted. Spoon the noodles and beansprouts into deep bowls, then ladle over the stock to serve. Eat whilst piping hot.

For non-vegans...

To make a simple version of this pho for meat eaters, replace the water in step 3 with 1 litre/35fl oz/4¼ cups hot good-quality beef stock, and add some very finely sliced steak to the soup when you add the vegetables.

2

LIGHT BITES
& LUNCHES

Marmite fingers

Be warned, these are incredibly moreish – the Marmite taste is subtle – just enough to flavour. You can use whatever seeds you like but I've just used a mix of white and black sesame seeds. The quantity depends on how you break up the fingers but you'll make enough to cover two baking/cookie sheets.

Makes about 50
Prep: 15 mins Cook: 15 mins

200g/7oz/1⅔ cups plain/all-purpose
    flour, sifted, plus extra for dusting
1 tbsp caster/superfine sugar
¼ tsp baking powder, sifted
¼ tsp sea salt
50g/1¾oz sunflower spread,
    refrigerator cold
1 tsp Marmite mixed with a tiny
    drizzle of warm water
juice of ¼ lemon
4 tbsp almond milk
2 tsp black sesame seeds
2 tsp sesame seeds

1 Put the flour, sugar, baking powder and salt in a bowl and mix together. Add the sunflower spread and rub it in with your fingertips until the mixture resembles breadcrumbs.

2 Trickle in the Marmite and water and mix to combine, then squeeze the lemon juice into the almond milk and add it to the bowl a little at a time until the ingredients come together as dough. Wrap the dough in cling film/plastic wrap and put it in the refrigerator for at least 20 minutes, or overnight if you have time.

3 Preheat the oven to 200°C/400°F/Gas 6 and line two baking/cookie sheets with parchment paper.

4 When ready to bake, turn the dough out onto a lightly floured surface and cut it in half. Roll out the first half as thinly as it will go to a large rectangle about 38 x 40cm/15 x 16in, then carefully transfer it to a prepared baking/cookie sheet by draping it over your rolling pin. Put it in the refrigerator to chill while you prepare the other half of dough in the same way. Scatter half the seeds over each piece and gently press them in.

5 Bake for about 15 minutes until golden. Leave to cool, then slice or break into fingers. They will keep in an airtight container for up to a week.

For non-vegans...
These Marmite fingers go very well with a mackerel or salmon pâté.

Fennel & miso crackers

I always think that anything made with spelt flour sounds a little worthy, but it does add a nice nutty backdrop. These crackers are light and very addictive! The miso gives an umami flavour, which makes them gutsy enough to eat on their own. Adding a little lemon juice to the soy milk sours it slightly so it is rather like buttermilk. Top with whatever takes your fancy – some steamed asparagus blitzed with soy yogurt to make a pâté is rather nice. You can buy red miso in large supermarkets or Asian stores, but Marmite would also work.

Makes about 80 small squares
Prep: 20 mins Cook: 15 mins

a little sunflower spread, for greasing
400g/14oz/3¼ cups spelt flour, sifted, plus extra for dusting
½ tsp baking powder
a pinch of caster/superfine sugar
a pinch of sea salt, plus extra for topping (optional)
3 tsp fennel seeds
1 tsp caraway seeds
½ tsp black peppercorns, cracked in a pestle and mortar
1 tsp red miso paste
100ml/3½fl oz/scant ½ cup soy milk
juice of ½ lemon

1 Preheat the oven to 200°C/400°F/Gas 6 and grease or line two baking/cookie sheets with parchment paper.

2 Put the flour, baking powder, sugar and salt into a bowl and stir to combine, then stir in the fennel and caraway seeds and the pepper.

3 Put the miso paste in a measuring jug and add 100ml/3½fl oz/scant ½ cup of boiling water from the kettle, the soy milk and lemon juice and mix well. Slowly pour the mixture into the flour and beat it together to form a dough. If it is too wet, add a little more flour.

4 Turn the dough out onto a lightly floured surface and cut it in half. Roll out the first half as thinly as it will go to a large rectangle about 38 x 40cm/15 x 16in, then carefully transfer it to a prepared baking/cookie sheet by draping it over your rolling pin. Score it into slices or small squares and put it in the refrigerator to chill while you prepare the other half of dough in the same way.

5 Bake the crackers for 15 minutes, or until golden and crisp. Remove from oven and leave to cool, then slice apart to serve. They will keep in an airtight container or lidded tin for up to 4 days.

For non-vegans...
You could add a couple of tablespoons of finely grated Parmesan cheese into the dry mixture.

Apple soda bread

You don't have to be a great baker to make soda bread. It is the easiest of breads to make as it very forgiving and little can go wrong. You don't require a loaf pan as it is freeform and it takes very little time to make and bake. It is best eaten on the day of baking, so a good bread to make if friends are coming over to share a meal. Pictured overleaf.

Makes 1 x 450g/1lb loaf
Prep: 15 mins Cook: 50 mins

375g/13oz/3 cups plain/all-purpose flour (or use a mix of 200g/7oz/ scant 1⅔ cups plain/all-purpose flour and 175g/6oz/scant 1½ cups wholemeal flour), sifted, plus extra for dusting
½ tsp bicarbonate of soda/baking soda, sifted
a pinch of sea salt
200g/7oz/scant 1 cup soy yogurt
100ml/3½fl oz/scant ½ cup soy milk
juice of ½ lemon
1 tbsp dark treacle/molasses
2 small or 1 large eating/dessert apples, peeled, cored and grated

1 Preheat the oven 200°C/400°F/Gas 6 and line a baking/ cookie sheet with parchment paper.

2 Put the flour, bicarbonate of soda/baking soda and salt in a large bowl and stir to combine. Put the yogurt, milk, lemon juice and treacle/molasses in a jug and stir to combine.

3 Make a well in the middle of the flour mixture and gradually pour in the yogurt mixture, blending them together as you go, then stir in the apple.

4 Tip the mixture out onto a lightly floured surface and, using floured hands, shape it into a round. Handle the dough as briefly as you can. It is nothing like regular dough. The mixture is fairly sticky but just dust the board and your hands well and add a little more flour, if needed, until it comes together as a ball. Slash the top with a large cross, about 1cm/½in deep.

5 Bake for about 45–50 minutes. When it is cooked, the loaf should be golden and knobbly and the base should feel hollow when tapped. Leave to cool on a wire rack for 5–10 minutes, then slice and serve warm.

For non-vegans...
You can use dairy yogurt and buttermilk instead of the soy milk if you prefer. A piece of Stilton cheese and some chutney would make a delicious accompaniment to this bread.

Rye bread with a trio of toppings

An incredibly easy bread to rustle up – you can halve the rye flour and mix with another type of flour if you want a lighter bread but I prefer the full-on rye flavour. The trio of toppings makes this a *smørrebrød* – a type of Danish open sandwich that usually has a meat or fish topping but here works brilliantly with vegetable and fruit. Pictured overleaf.

Makes 1 x 600g/1lb 5oz loaf
Prep: 10 mins Cook: 35 mins

250g/9oz/2 cups rye flour, sifted,
  plus extra for dusting
1 tsp bicarbonate of soda/baking
  soda
100g/3½oz/heaped ¾ cup
  mixed seeds, such as
  pumpkin, sunflower, linseed
  and sesame seeds
sea salt
100g/3½oz/scant 1 cup soy yogurt
100ml/3½fl oz/scant ½ cup almond
  milk
100ml/3½fl oz/scant ½ cup
  rapeseed oil, plus extra for
  greasing
1 tbsp maple syrup

FOR THE TOPPINGS
hummus, sliced avocado, sliced
  beetroot/beet, sliced radishes,
  snipped chives
almond butter, halved strawberries,
  halved raspberries, sliced
  banana, mint leaves
sliced cooked new potatoes,
  watercress, chopped dill, thinly
  sliced red onion, mustard and
  alfalfa sprouts

1 Preheat the oven to 200°C/400°F/Gas 6 and have ready a 900g/2lb loaf pan.

2 Put the flour, bicarbonate of soda/baking soda, seed mixture and a pinch of salt into a large bowl. Put the yogurt, almond milk, oil and maple syrup in a jug and stir to combine. Make a well in the middle of the flour mixture and gradually pour in the yogurt mixture, blending them together as you go. The mixture will be fairly wet.

3 Turn the dough out onto a lightly floured surface and knead it gently, then transfer it to the loaf pan and level the top. Sit the pan on a baking/cookie sheet and bake for 25–35 minutes until golden and the base feels hollow when tapped. Leave to cool slightly, and serve warm or leave to cool completely. Slice to serve and eat on its own or with toppings of your choice.

For non-vegans...

To create a traditional *smørrebrød*, top with smoked salmon, pickled radish and dill or Stilton with pear and walnuts.

Sweet potato, ginger & wasabi soup

This is a simple and warming soup but one that packs a punch and is perfect for the colder months. I can only cope with a light hint of wasabi but ramp it up if you like it hotter.

Serves 4
Prep: 15 mins Cook: 30 mins

1 tbsp olive oil
1 onion, finely chopped
2 garlic cloves, finely chopped
5cm/1¾in piece of fresh root ginger, peeled and grated
5 sweet potatoes (about 700g/1lb 9oz), peeled and chopped into even-sized pieces
¼ tsp wasabi (use less or more depending how hot you like it – but remember it packs a punch)
1 litre/35fl oz/4¼ cups hot vegetable stock
sea salt and freshly ground black pepper
soy yogurt, to serve
a few chives, finely snipped, to garnish (optional)

1 Heat the oil in a large, heavy-based pan. Add the onion, season with salt and pepper and cook for 2–3 minutes until softened. Stir in the garlic and ginger and cook for a few seconds more.

2 Add the sweet potatoes and wasabi and turn so they are all coated in the flavoured oil, then cook for a couple of minutes. Pour in a little stock, raise the heat and let it bubble for a minute, then pour in the remaining stock. Cook over a high heat for a few minutes until bubbling, then turn the heat down and simmer with the lid on for about 20–25 minutes, or until the potatoes are fork tender.

3 Remove from the heat, ladle into a blender and whiz until smooth. Taste and season as it needs it. Transfer to serving bowls, add a dollop of yogurt, give it a swirl and scatter over the chives, if using, to serve.

For non-vegans...

Add a portion of cooked garlic prawns/shrimp after blending, and heat through before serving. Alternatively, top the soup with sour cream

Mushroom & cider soup

I think mushroom soup, warm crusty bread and a glass of cider is heaven for a cold day. I always prefer to use chestnut/cremini mushrooms rather than white mushrooms for soup as I think they have a deeper and more earthy flavour. Cider complements the ingredients perfectly – plus it's even better to have some left over to drink.

Serves 4
Prep: 15 mins Cook: 30 mins

1 tbsp olive oil
1 onion, finely chopped
1 leek, trimmed and finely chopped
2 garlic cloves, finely chopped
a few thyme leaves
700g/1½lb chestnut/cremini
    mushrooms, chopped
200ml/7fl oz/scant 1 cup dry cider
1.1 litres/38fl oz/4⅔ cups hot
    vegetable stock
100ml/3½fl oz/scant ½ cup almond
    milk (optional)
a pinch of freshly grated nutmeg
sea salt and freshly grated black
    pepper

1 Heat the oil in a large, heavy-based pan. Add the onion, season well with salt and pepper and cook for 2–3 minutes until softened. Stir in the leek and garlic and cook for a few minutes more until the leek starts to soften.

2 Add the thyme and mushrooms, stir and cook over a low heat for a few minutes until the mushrooms start to release their juices. Raise the heat to high, add the cider and bubble for a few minutes, stirring so everything is coated, then pour in the stock and continue cooking on a high heat until the soup is boiling nicely, then turn the heat down and simmer for about 20 minutes until all the ingredients are tender.

3 Remove from the heat, pour the soup into a blender and whiz until smooth, then return it to the pan and add the milk, if using. Heat it through and add a pinch of nutmeg before serving.

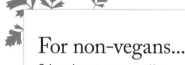

For non-vegans...

Crispy bacon or pancetta makes a delicious topping to this soup. Melt a knob of butter in a frying pan, add some chopped bacon pieces or pancetta and fry for 2–3 minutes until crispy, then sprinkle over the top of the soup before serving.

Tomato, lime & coconut soup with garlic toast

This is a great soup to make in summer when tomatoes are really flavoursome. Don't overdo the lime – it just needs to add a little zing, not too much acidity. If you really hate the tomato skins, rub the soup through a sieve/fine-mesh strainer once you have liquidized it. And if you prefer using a low-fat coconut milk, keep a careful eye on it and don't raise the heat too much as it is more likely to split.

Serves 4
Prep: 10 mins Cook: 30 mins

1 tbsp olive oil
1 onion, finely chopped
2 garlic cloves, finely chopped
a pinch of freshly grated nutmeg
8 tomatoes, roughly chopped
1 tbsp tomato purée/paste
1.2 litres/40fl oz/5 cups hot
    vegetable stock
2 x 400ml/14fl oz cans of
    coconut milk
juice of ½–1 lime
1 small handful of fresh coconut
    chunks
a few chives, to garnish
sea salt and freshly ground black
    pepper

FOR THE TOAST
chunky slices of sourdough or Apple
    Soda Bread (see page 40)
a drizzle of olive oil
1–2 large garlic cloves, halved

1 Heat the oil in a large saucepan, add the onion and cook for 2–3 minutes until soft. Add the garlic, season with salt and pepper and cook for a minute more. Sprinkle in the nutmeg, add the tomatoes and tomato purée/paste and stir to coat. Raise the heat and add a little stock, bubble it for a minute, then add the remaining stock and the coconut milk. Bring it all to the boil, then turn the heat down and simmer gently, partially covered with a lid, for about 20 minutes.

2 Squeeze in a little lime juice, taste and season some more if needed. While the soup is cooking, preheat the oven to 200°C/400°F/Gas 6.

3 Put the coconut chunks on a baking/cookie sheet and cook for about 6–8 minutes, or until golden. Or you could toss them in a hot griddle pan for a few minutes until golden and toasted. Shred the coconut carefully with a sharp knife into fine shards, then leave to one side.

4 Heat a griddle pan to hot. Drizzle the sliced bread with olive oil and rub with garlic. Put them in the griddle pan and cook for about 5 minutes on each side until char lines appear. Rub the bread with more garlic and add a sprinkling of salt.

5 Transfer the soup to serving bowls, top with toasted coconut and a few chives and serve with the garlic toast.

For non-vegans...
Top the soup with some fresh crab meat, or serve the crab on toast as an accompaniment.

Avocado, spinach & chipotle mushroom tortilla

This is a just like a quesadilla although since *queso* means cheese, I couldn't really call it that. Creamy avocado contrasts perfectly with the chipotle chillies, which are dried and smoked jalapeño chillies that add a deep, smoky accent to your food. You'll find chipotle paste with the spices at the supermarket. If you like, you could use any mixture of exotic mushrooms, and also toss in some fresh, roughly chopped tomatoes to the mix if you have them.

Makes 4
Prep: 15 mins Cook: 20 mins

1 tbsp olive oil
2 red onions, roughly chopped
2 garlic cloves, roughly chopped
1–2 tbsp chipotle paste
400g/14oz mushrooms, sliced
8 flour or corn tortillas
200g/7oz spinach leaves
2–3 avocados, pitted and sliced
sea salt and freshly ground black
    pepper
1 handful of coriander/cilantro
    leaves, chopped, plus extra to
    garnish
lime wedges, to serve

1 Heat the oil in a large frying pan. Add the onions, season with salt and pepper and cook for 2–3 minutes until beginning to soften. Stir in the garlic and cook for a few seconds more. Stir in the chipotle paste and let it bubble for a minute, then add the mushrooms and toss them around the pan. Cook for about 3–4 minutes until tender. Remove from the heat.

2 Heat a griddle pan to hot, add the tortillas one at a time and cook for a few seconds to warm.

3 Meanwhile, rinse the spinach and put in a bowl with just the water clinging to the leaves. Microwave for 2–3 minutes until wilted.

4 Spoon the mushrooms, wilted spinach and avocado onto four of the warmed tortillas, top with a few coriander/cilantro leaves then put another tortilla on top of each to make a sandwich. Carefully put one tortilla back in the hot griddle pan, squash down to flatten, and heat through for a minute. Turn and cook the other side for the same time. Repeat with the other tortillas. Slice each tortilla into four, garnish with coriander/cilantro and serve with lime wedges.

For non-vegans...

To make this into a quesadilla, add some crumbled feta or grated strong cheddar to the filling. These tortillas also make a wonderful accompaniment to roast chicken.

Garlic sourdough with courgette & tomato salsa

Such an easy lunch or snack to pull together but with great flavours. I think griddling courgettes/zucchini is the best cooking method for them as they become sweet and smoky. A nice way to serve this is to put your garlic clove on a cocktail stick so you can rub it over the toast yourself, with the courgettes/zucchini and salsa on the side, ready to assemble.

Serves 2–4
Prep: 15 mins Cook: 20 mins

4 chunky slices of sourdough or
  Apple Soda Bread (see page 40)
  made with spelt or ordinary flour
a drizzle of extra virgin olive oil
2 garlic cloves, peeled

**FOR THE CHILLI COURGETTES/
ZUCCHINI**
about 3–4 courgettes/zucchini,
  trimmed and finely sliced
  lengthways
a drizzle of extra virgin olive oil
a pinch of chilli flakes
zest and juice of ½ lemon

FOR THE TOMATO SALSA
4 ripe and juicy tomatoes, chopped
2 spring onions/scallions, trimmed
  and finely chopped
juice of 1 lime
½–1 green chilli (depending on your
  heat preference), deseeded and
  finely chopped
1 handful of coriander/cilantro
  leaves, chopped
sea salt and freshly ground black
  pepper

1 First make the salsa so it can sit and allow the flavours to develop while you prepare the rest of the recipe. Put all the salsa ingredients in a bowl, mix well and season to taste with salt and pepper. Leave the salsa to stand for at least an hour, if you can, for the flavours to develop.

2 To cook the courgettes/zucchini, put them in a shallow dish, drizzle over the oil to coat but not soak, season with salt and pepper and add the chilli and lemon zest and juice. Shake the dish or stir them around so they are well mixed. Leave to stand for 15 minutes, if you have time.

3 Heat a griddle pan to hot, add a few courgette/zucchini strips at a time so you don't overcrowd the pan and cook for a minute or so, or until the underside begins to show char lines, then turn and cook the other side. Repeat until all the courgettes/zucchini are cooked.

4 While the griddle pan is still hot, it shouldn't need cleaning. Add the bread two slices at a time and cook for a minute or so until char lines appear, then turn and cook the other side. Remove from the pan, drizzle with the extra virgin olive oil and rub liberally with the garlic. Place a slice of bread on each serving plate, pile the courgettes/zucchini on top and serve with a spoonful of salsa. Be prepared for it to all dribble down your chin!

Quick-fix salad with ginger & miso dressing

I call this a quick fix because it restores you! It makes you feel virtuous, as it's so full of the good stuff. It's like a detox in a bowl. There is no cooking required – all it needs is a vibrant dressing to pull it all together. It also makes a great lunch on the go, in which case pack the dressing separately and add it when you are ready to eat.

Serves 2–4
Prep: 20 mins

4 carrots, grated

4 raw beetroot/beet, peeled and grated (discard the first outer bits)

1 raw orange beetroot/beet, peeled and finely sliced

1 fennel bulb, trimmed and very finely sliced

2 eating/dessert apples, cored and very finely sliced

1 large handful of baby spinach leaves

1 large handful of sprouting beans (optional)

1 handful of ready-to-eat pitted dates, finely chopped

1 handful of coriander/cilantro leaves, chopped

1 handful of sunflower seeds, toasted, for topping

FOR THE DRESSING

6 tbsp extra virgin olive oil

2 tbsp cider vinegar

1–2 tsp red miso paste

5cm/1¾in piece of fresh root ginger, peeled and grated

juice of ½ orange

sea salt and freshly ground black pepper

1 First make the dressing. Mix together the oil and vinegar and season well with salt and pepper. Whisk in the miso, adding a little to start with as it can be quite an overpowering taste, then add the ginger and orange juice and mix well. Adjust the seasoning to taste, adding more miso, orange juice, salt or pepper. Leave to one side.

2 Put all the salad ingredients, except the coriander/cilantro and sunflower seeds, in a large bowl and toss to combine. Drizzle over the dressing, then tumble it all together so everything is coated. Stir in the coriander/cilantro, transfer to serving bowls and sprinkle over the seeds to serve.

For non-vegans...

To add a little more protein, toss some shredded poached chicken in with the rest of the salad ingredients.

Falafel wraps with yogurt dip

These take a bit of time, although using canned chickpeas/garbanzos speeds it up. They should be a nice 'fluffy' texture when cooked. This makes plenty of falafels as I don't see the point in all the work for just a few, so put any leftovers in a sealed container and keep in the refrigerator for up to three days.

Makes about 30 falafels
Prep: 30 mins, plus chilling
Cook: 20 mins

2 x 400g/14oz cans of chickpeas/
    garbanzos, drained
1 onion, roughly chopped
3 garlic cloves, roughly chopped
1–2 tsp ground cumin (depending
    on how much you like the taste)
1 tsp ground coriander
1 handful of flatleaf parsley leaves,
    chopped
about 2–3 tbsp plain/all-purpose
    flour, sifted, plus extra for dusting
sunflower/rapeseed oil, for deep-frying
wraps of your choice
baby cos/romaine lettuce, trimmed
    and torn
4–6 tomatoes, roughly chopped
lemon wedges, to serve
sea salt and freshly ground black
    pepper

FOR THE YOGURT DIP
1 handful of mint leaves, finely
    chopped
500g/1lb 2oz/2¼ cup soy yogurt

For non-vegans...
Add 200g/8oz minced/
ground lamb to the mixture in
step 2 to make lamb falafel.

1 Line a baking/cookie sheet with parchment paper.

2 Put the chickpeas/garbanzos, onion, garlic, cumin and coriander in a food processor, season with salt and pepper and whiz to combine. Add the parsley and whiz again so you have a thick paste. Taste and season some more if needed. Scrape the mixture into a bowl, tip in the flour and mix together. You may need to add more flour later.

3 With wet hands, scoop up a walnut-sized ball and lightly roll. If the mixture seems too wet, add a little more flour, but be careful not to add too much. Repeat until you have used all the mixture, placing the balls on the prepared baking/cookie sheet, and put in the refrigerator to chill for a couple of hours.

4 To make the yogurt dip, stir the mint into the yogurt, season to taste with salt and pepper and mix well. Put in the refrigerator until needed.

5 Add the oil to a large pan or deep-frying pan – it needs to be 5cm/1¾in deep. Heat the oil to 180°C/350°F, or when a small cube of bread sizzles immediately when dropped into the oil. If the balls are not very firm, roll them lightly in flour before frying. Add just a few balls at a time otherwise the temperature of the oil will drop and they won't cook as well or as evenly. Lower them into the oil using a slotted spoon, and cook for about 3 minutes each side, or until golden all over. Drain on paper towels while you fry the rest.

6 Fill each wrap with a handful of crisp lettuce leaves, 2–3 falafels, some tomato pieces and a dollop of mint yogurt. Add a squeeze of lemon, then roll up and enjoy.

Mezze platter

The best kind of food for informal eating or good for the lunch box, here's a party of many small foods that you can pick and mix from or make them all. I've mixed up the cuisines a little here, with Mediterranean vegetables and Middle Eastern grains and hummus – all you need to add is some olives, bread and wine.

Serves 4–6
Prep: 30 mins Cook: 30 mins

FOR THE TABBOULEH
100g/3½ oz/heaped ½ cup bulgar
    wheat, rinsed
about 6 tomatoes, deseeded and
    finely diced
4 spring onions/scallions, trimmed
    and finely chopped
juice of ½ lemon
1 large handful of flatleaf parsley
    leaves, chopped
1 large handful of mint leaves,
    chopped
sea salt and freshly ground black
    pepper

FOR THE HUMMUS
2 x 400g/14oz cans of chickpeas/
    garbanzos, drained, juice
    reserved to use in baking
    (see page 16)
about 3 tbsp tahini
juice of ½–1 lemon
a couple of pinches of paprika
2 garlic cloves, crushed
about 3 tbsp extra virgin olive oil

FOR THE GRIDDLED VEG
4 red peppers, halved, deseeded
    and roughly chopped
4 courgettes/zucchini, trimmed and
    sliced lengthways
extra virgin olive oil

1 The tabbouleh is all about the herbs so add plenty. Put the bulgar wheat in a pan, cover with water to about 2.5cm/1in above the bulgar and add a pinch of salt. Bring to the boil, then simmer for about 10 minutes, or until all water has been absorbed and the bulgar is tender. Drain into a bowl and fluff up with a fork. Add the tomatoes, spring onions/scallions, lemon juice and herbs and season well with salt and pepper.

2 To make the hummus, put the chickpeas/garbanzos in a food processor with the tahini and lemon juice and whiz to combine. With the motor running, add a pinch of paprika and the garlic and trickle in the olive oil, then begin to add about 6 tablespoons of hot water until the hummus reaches the consistency you prefer. You can make it as smooth or textured as you wish. Taste and season some more if needed. Transfer to a serving dish and drizzle with a little more oil and a pinch of paprika.

3 To cook the vegetables, brush the peppers and courgettes/zucchini with a little oil and season well with salt and pepper. Heat a griddle pan until it is hot, then add the vegetables, a few at a time, and cook for a few minutes on each side until char lines appear. Transfer to a serving plate.

Prepare any other ingredients of your choice. Among my favourites are: mixed olives, sliced radishes, cherry tomatoes cucumber, cut into sticks, warm flatbreads, Falafel Wraps with Yogurt Dip (see page 52)

Sort of vegetable sushi

This is a mix of all the flavours in sushi but deconstructed so it's quick and easy with no cooking, rather than involving fiddly techniques.

Serves 2
Prep: 20 mins Cook: 30 mins

200g/7oz/scant 1 cup sushi rice
about ½–1 tbsp rice vinegar
1–2 sheets dried nori, finely
    shredded
1 large carrot, cut into matchsticks
1 avocado, pitted and sliced, then
    tossed in lemon or lime juice to
    stop it from discolouring
½ cucumber, halved lengthways,
    deseeded and cut into sticks
1 handful of radishes, sliced or cut
    into matchsticks
1 mango, halved, pitted and cubed
about 150g/5oz/1¼ cups ready-
    cooked marinated tofu
sea salt and freshly ground black
    pepper

FOR THE WASABI DRESSING
3 tbsp dark soy sauce
2 tbsp rice vinegar
1 tsp grated fresh root ginger
2 tsp caster/superfine sugar
1–2 tsp wasabi (depending on how
    hot you like it)
a drizzle of sesame oil

TO SERVE
toasted sesame seeds or black
    sesame seeds
a few shiso leaves (optional)
about 1 tbsp pickled ginger
lime wedges

1 Put the rice in a pan, add twice as much water and a pinch of salt and bring to the boil. Turn the heat down and simmer with the lid on for about 25–30 minutes, or until tender and the water has been absorbed. Remove from the heat and keep the lid on for the rice to steam for a few minutes. Mix in the rice vinegar and nori and season to taste with salt. Transfer to a serving bowl and leave to one side.

2 To make the wasabi dressing, mix all the ingredients together, then adjust the seasoning to taste.

3 Arrange on plates or bowls to serve the rice with the carrot, avocado, cucumber, radishes, mango and tofu sprinkled with black sesame seeds and shiso, with the pickled ginger, wasabi dressing and lime wedges on the side.

For non-vegans...
The flavours of this sushi-inspired salad mean it goes very well with fish. Try serving it with some slices of smoked salmon and fresh white crab meat.

Pot noodle

This is just a lazy no-cook noodle dish. You can layer everything up in a pot or large jar, which is great to take to work with you to give you a day off from sandwiches. Or, of course, pile everything into bowls and dig in. Add whatever veg you like as long as it doesn't really need cooking and choose noodles that just need hot water for a couple of minutes to cook. You could stir in chopped mint and coriander/cilantro at the end, if you wish.

Serves 2
Prep: 5 mins Cook: 5 mins

2 nests of vermicelli rice noodles or
    egg-free noodles of your choice
1 large handful of frozen peas,
    defrosted
1 large handful of beansprouts
1 tsp ground turmeric
1 red chilli, deseeded and finely
    chopped
5cm/1¾in piece of fresh root ginger,
    peeled and grated
1 handful of mushrooms, sliced
1 large handful of baby spinach
    leaves
a splash of toasted sesame oil
1 tbsp rice wine vinegar mixed with
    1–2 tsp demerara/turbinado
    sugar
2 tsp black rice vinegar or a splash
    of balsamic vinegar
a splash of dark soy sauce
juice of 1 lime
sea salt and freshly ground black
    pepper

1 Layer the noodles, peas, beansprouts, turmeric, chilli, ginger, mushrooms and spinach in a pot or bowl. Mix together the sesame oil, rice vinegars, soy sauce and lime and season well with salt and pepper.

2 When ready to serve, add the oil and vinegar mix to the vegetables and pour over just enough boiling water to cover, stir well and leave to stand for at least 5 minutes, or until the flavours mingle and the noodles are tender. Adjust the seasoning to taste, adding more soy sauce, lime juice, salt or pepper.

For non-vegans...
This pot noodle is a wonderful vehicle for leftover meats like shredded cooked chicken. Alternatively, add a few cooked prawns/ shrimp or chopped hard-boiled egg.

Asian sticky rice pot

Rice simmered in coconut milk is sublime. My apologies that it increases the calories but if this is a worry, use plain boiled rice. White rice sometimes just works better and I think that this is one of those times, but again if you prefer brown rice, use it. You'll find the sweet Indonesian sauce, kecap manis, in Asian stores – a thick and sugary soy sauce that's a great condiment for stir-fries.

Serves 4
Prep: 10 mins Cook: 20 mins

200g/7oz/heaped 1 cup long-grain rice
200ml/7fl oz can of coconut milk
about 3 tbsp sesame oil
2 tbsp dark soy sauce
1 tbsp rice vinegar
a pinch of demerara/turbinado sugar
2 garlic cloves, grated
3 aubergines/eggplants, cut into chunky pieces
1 handful of frozen soy beans, defrosted
2–3 spring onions/scallions, trimmed and finely chopped
1 handful of sesame seeds, toasted (optional)
a drizzle of kecap manis sauce (optional)
sea salt and freshly ground black pepper

1 Put the rice in a pan and pour in the coconut milk, 200ml/7fl oz/scant 1 cup of water and a pinch of salt. Bring to the boil, then cover with the lid and cook for about 20 minutes, or until the rice has absorbed the liquid and is tender. Remove from the heat, keep the lid on and leave to one side.

2 While the rice is cooking, heat the sesame oil in a wok. Mix together the soy sauce, rice vinegar, sugar and garlic and toss with the aubergine/eggplant until coated. Add to the hot oil, and toss around the pan on a fairly high heat for 5–6 minutes until the aubergine/eggplant is tender and sticky.

3 Meanwhile, bring a pan of salted water to the boil, add the soy beans, then turn the heat down and simmer for about 4 minutes. Drain well, then add them to the aubergine/eggplant and stir to combine. Sprinkle over the spring onions/scallions and stir gently.

4 Serve the rice and aubergine/eggplant in layers in serving bowls and top with sesame seeds, if using. Finish with a small drizzle of kecap manis, if using.

For non-vegans...
Make this a traditional Nasi Goreng by adding some cooked, shredded chicken and cooked prawns/shrimp to the soup to heat through. Serve with a fried egg on top.

Peanut butter & ginger noodles

These are super-quick and really do hit the spot. It's the sort of food that you can't stop eating from the pan – we all do it! I won't deny these may be slightly high in fat due to the peanut butter but use one without added sugar and just don't eat them every day. I think this is the perfect rummage-through-the-storecupboard supper. You can swap the beans for whatever you have in the bottom of the fridge – mange tout/snow peas, sugar snaps or chopped courgettes/zucchini – as long as it is green and fresh to cut through the richness. Feel free to use any noodles but I think these thick ones have the perfect 'slurpabilty'.

Serves 2
Prep: 5 mins Cook: 15 mins

2 tbsp smooth sugar-free peanut
     butter
2 tbsp dark soy sauce
2 tbsp mirin/rice wine
juice of 1 lime
salt
180g/6¼oz fine green beans,
     trimmed and cut into three
1 tbsp olive oil
4 spring onions/scallions, trimmed
     and finely chopped
10cm/4in piece of fresh root ginger,
     peeled and grated
2 garlic cloves, finely chopped or
     grated
2 x 150g/5oz packs of straight-to-
     wok, thick udon noodles
1 handful of coriander/cilantro
     leaves, finely chopped
lime wedges, to serve

1 Mix together the peanut butter, soy sauce, mirin, lime juice and 1 tablespoon of hot water and leave to one side.

2 Bring a pan of salted water to the boil, add the beans and boil for 2–3 minutes; they should still be firm. Drain and refresh well in cold water, then leave to one side.

3 Heat the oil in a wok. Add the spring onions/scallions and cook for a couple of minutes, moving them around the pan. Add the ginger and garlic and cook for a minute more. Spoon in the peanut butter mixture and stir well, topping up with a little more hot water if you wish to thin it down. Add the noodles and mix so the noodles are coated, then stir in the beans and most of the coriander/cilantro. Divide into two serving bowls, sprinkle with the remaining coriander/cilantro and serve with lime wedges.

For non-vegans...

Thinly slice 200g/7oz beef rump steak, rub with oil and season with salt and pepper. Fry in a hot pan for 2–2½ minutes until cooked to your liking, and stir in to the noodles.

Quick miso soup with greens

This recipe is effortless, delicious and a great way to stave off mid-morning hunger pangs. I am a huge grazer and easily distracted, so a steaming bowl of this is a great way to keep me on track and locked to my desk, especially when I am up against a deadline.

Serves 2
Prep: 5 mins Cook: 5 mins

2–3 tbsp red miso (depending on
    how strong you like it)
a pinch of chilli flakes
2.5cm/1in piece of fresh root ginger,
    peeled and finely grated
1 large handful of spinach leaves,
    roughly chopped

1 Divide the miso between two bowls or mugs, pour over boiling water and whisk until it has dissolved. Stir in the chilli flakes and ginger, add the spinach and push it into the soup so it begins to wilt. Serve!

Walnut, spinach & tangerine pilaf

These one-pan wonders are the best sort of dishes to cook up as you can get so creative with the flavours. Here you get bitter, earthy and sweet. It may seem like a lot of onion but it really completes the dish. It's a pan full of nutritious goodness too! You could scatter some pomegranate seeds on top for added sweetness, if you like.

Serves 4
Prep: 15 mins Cook: 30 mins

2 tbsp sunflower spread
1 onion, finely chopped
2 garlic cloves, finely chopped
about 4–5 cardamom pods, crushed
2 tsp fennel seeds
350g/12oz/scant 2 cups basmati
  rice
900ml/31fl oz/3¾ cups hot
  vegetable stock
1 handful of spinach leaves
1 handful of walnuts, roughly
  chopped
2 tsp demerara/turbinado sugar
1 handful of flatleaf parsley leaves,
  finely chopped
3–4 tangerines, peeled and sliced or
  use orange segments

FOR THE THYME ONIONS

1 tbsp olive oil
4 red onions, very finely sliced
a few thyme stalks, leaves only
sea salt and freshly ground black
  pepper

1 To make the thyme onions, heat the oil in a frying pan. Add the onions, season with salt and pepper and give them a good stir. Add the thyme leaves and cook over a medium to high heat, stirring occasionally so they don't burn. Leave them to cook for about 20 minutes, or until they start to sweeten and caramelize. When ready, remove from the heat and leave to one side.

2 While the onions are cooking, in another large frying pan, heat the sunflower spread. Add the onion, season well with salt and pepper and cook for a couple of minutes to soften. Stir in the garlic, cardamom and fennel seeds and cook for a few seconds more. Stir in the rice, making sure it soaks up all the juices as you turn it. Pour in most of the stock and bring it to the boil, then turn the heat down and simmer for about 15–20 minutes, stirring occasionally. You can add more stock if you need to. Simmer until the rice is cooked and has absorbed all the liquid. Stir in the spinach, cover with a lid and put it to one side to let it steam a little and allow the spinach to wilt.

3 Meanwhile, put the walnuts and sugar in a small frying pan and cook for a few minutes until the sugar is golden and the walnuts are coated. Remove from the heat and leave to one side.

4 Taste and season some more if needed. To serve, stir in half the parsley, then pile on the tangerines or orange segments, walnuts and onions, then scatter with remaining parsley.

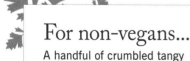

For non-vegans...
A handful of crumbled tangy feta would work its magic on top of this dish.

3

WEEKNIGHT
SUPPERS

Tarka dahl

When this is spiced to perfection, it is one of the most satisfying things to eat and you can keep going at it bowl after bowl. I like topping it with roasted tomatoes for an extra boost of sweetness but this is because I often have tomatoes that need using up. If you don't have any tomatoes to hand, serve it alone and it will be just as delicious – but, a roti is essential for scooping. Pictured overleaf, right.

Serve 4
Prep: 10 mins Cook: 1 hour

400g/14oz/heaped 2 cups mung dahl (yellow split mung beans), rinsed well
1 tbsp olive oil
1 onion, finely chopped
2 garlic cloves, finely chopped
5cm/1¾in piece of fresh root ginger, peeled and grated
2 tsp ground turmeric
2 tsp mustard seeds
a pinch of chilli flakes
400g/14oz can of plum tomatoes
1 handful of coriander/cilantro
rotis, warmed, to serve
cooked white rice, to serve (optional)
sea salt and freshly ground black pepper

FOR THE ROAST TOMATO TOPPING
about 4–6 tomatoes, quartered
a drizzle of olive oil

1 Put the mung beans in a large pan, add a pinch of salt and just cover with water. Bring to the boil over a high heat, then turn the heat down and simmer for about 20 minutes, or until thick, sloppy and the beans are soft. You will need to skim away and discard any scum that comes to the top of the pan.

2 While the mung beans are cooking, preheat the oven to 190°C/375°F/Gas 5.

3 To make the roast tomato topping, put the fresh tomatoes in a roasting pan, drizzle over the oil and season well with salt and pepper. Roast for about 30–40 minutes, or until the tomatoes are charred and sweet.

4 Meanwhile, heat the oil in a large pan, add the onion, season with salt and pepper and cook for 2–3 minutes until beginning to soften. Stir in the garlic and ginger and cook for a minute more. Stir in the turmeric, mustard seeds and chilli flakes.

5 Add the canned tomatoes and bring to the boil, then turn the heat down, add the cooked dahl and simmer with the lid partially on for about 30 minutes, topping up with hot water from the kettle as necessary. It should be the consistency of soup. Taste and season some more if needed.

6 Top with the coriander/cilantro and serve with a pile of warmed roti and some plain white rice, if you like.

Green bean & tomato laksa

This is a bowl of glorious fragrance and colour. You can swap the vegetables to suit the seasons, or add some fried tofu cubes, but I like to keep it simple and light with just a couple of summery vegetables. It's all about getting the seasoning right: sweet and salty with a subtle sour note. Pictured overleaf, left.

Serves 4
Prep: 15 mins Cook: 30 mins

1 tbsp vegetable oil
400ml/14fl oz can of coconut milk
1 tsp demerara/turbinado sugar
500ml/17fl oz/generous 2 cups hot
   vegetable stock
juice of ½–1 lime
200g/7oz fine green beans, trimmed
   and cut into three
1 handful of cherry tomatoes
300g/10½oz vermicelli rice noodles,
   soaked in boiling water for
   3 minutes then drained
1 handful of bean sprouts
1 handful of coriander/cilantro
   leaves
1 handful of basil leaves to garnish
¼ cucumber, sliced lengthways,
   deseeded and sliced into half
   moons (optional)
line wedges, to serve

FOR THE SPICE MIX
1–3 red chillies, deseeded (depends
   on your heat preference)
3 shallots
2 garlic cloves
2.5cm/1in piece of fresh root ginger,
   peeled and chopped
1 lemongrass stalk, trimmed and
   peeled
1 tsp ground turmeric
1 tsp coriander seeds

1 First make the spice mix. Put all the spice mix ingredients in a food processor and whiz until finely chopped and the mixture becomes a paste.

2 Heat the oil over a medium heat in a large, heavy-based pan, add the spice mix and cook for a couple of minutes, stirring, then raise the heat and pour in a little of the coconut milk. Give it a stir and let it bubble, then add the remaining coconut milk. Turn the heat down and simmer for 5 minutes, stirring occasionally. Stir the sugar into the stock, then add it to the pan with the lime juice. Season well with salt and pepper and simmer gently for 10 minutes.

3 While the coconut sauce is cooking, bring a pan of salted water to the boil, add the green beans and cook for about 5–6 minutes until just tender. Drain and refresh in cold water until cool enough to handle. Add the beans to the pan with the tomatoes and cook for 10 minutes more, or until the tomatoes start to burst. Taste and season some more if needed, tinkering with the salt, lime or sugar until it is just right.

4 Stir in the noodles, half the bean sprouts and half the coriander/cilantro. Serve in individual bowls, topped with the remaining beansprouts and coriander/cilantro, the basil leaves, cucumber and lime wedges to serve.

For non-vegans...
Some large juicy prawns/shrimp or fresh mussels would be the perfect addition, or add one shelled, soft-boiled egg per person, if you want a vegetarian version.

Chunky bean soup with avocado & yogurt mash

Depending on how thick you make it, this delicious dish is on the border between a soup and a casserole. It tastes even better reheated the next day so it is a good one to make ahead.

Serves 4
Prep: 10 mins Cook: 1 hour

1 tbsp olive oil
1 red onion, finely chopped
2 garlic cloves, finely chopped
a pinch of dried oregano
1 bay leaf
2 carrots, diced
2 celery stalks, finely diced
a few rosemary stalks, leaves finely
    chopped
1 glass of white wine (about
    150ml/5fl oz/scant ⅔ cup)
400g/14oz can of plum tomatoes
400g/14oz can of borlotti beans,
    drained
400g/14oz can of chickpeas/
    garbanzos, drained, juice
    reserved to use in baking (see
    page 16)
500ml/17fl oz/generous 2 cups hot
    vegetable stock
1 handful of fine green beans,
    trimmed and cut into three
sea salt and freshly ground black
    pepper
1 handful of coriander/cilantro, finely
    chopped
warm crusty bread, to serve

FOR THE AVOCADO MASH
2 avocados, halved and pitted
about 2 tbsp soy yogurt with almond
    or plain soy yogurt
a drizzle of extra virgin olive oil, plus
    extra to serve

1 Heat the oil over a medium heat in a large, heavy-based pan, add the onion, season with salt and pepper and cook for 2–3 minutes until the onion has softened. Stir in the garlic and cook for a few seconds. Stir in the oregano, bay leaf, carrots, celery and rosemary and cook for 10 minutes, stirring occasionally, until the carrots begin to soften. Raise the heat a little, add the wine and let it bubble for a minute, then turn the heat down to low and add the tomatoes, breaking them up with a wooden spoon. Add the beans, chickpeas/garbanzos and stock. Bring to the boil, then turn the heat down and simmer with the lid partially on for about 25 minutes, topping up with hot water from the kettle if needed. Add the green beans and cook for 15 minutes more. Taste and season some more if needed.

2 To make the avocado mash, put the avocados, yogurt and olive oil in a bowl and season well with salt and pepper. Mash together just enough that it still remains chunky. Taste and season some more if needed.

3 Serve the soup with a little of the avocado mash spooned on the top, and finished with a drizzle of oil and a sprinkle of coriander/cilantro. Serve with some warm crusty bread on the side.

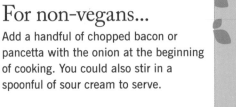

For non-vegans...
Add a handful of chopped bacon or pancetta with the onion at the beginning of cooking. You could also stir in a spoonful of sour cream to serve.

Potato, chickpea & peanut tamarind curry

This is fusion of tamarind, coconut and tomato and it works beautifully. You can control the heat by increasing or decreasing the number of chillies you add. It seems like a lot of ingredients but most of them will be in the storecupboard or refrigerator already.

Serves 4
Prep: 20 mins Cook: 30 mins

FOR THE SPICE MIX
1 tbsp coriander seeds
1 tsp cumin seeds
1 tsp black peppercorns
1–2 red chillies
1 tsp mustard seeds

FOR THE SAUCE
2 tbsp vegetable oil
1 onion, finely chopped
5cm/1¾in piece of fresh root ginger, peeled and grated
3 garlic cloves, grated
1 tsp ground turmeric
1 tsp garam masala
2 tbsp tamarind paste
400g/14oz can of plum tomatoes
400ml/14fl oz can of coconut milk
400g/14oz can of chickpeas/ garbanzos, drained
3 potatoes, peeled and cut into small pieces
100g/3½ oz/¾ cup frozen peas, defrosted
1 large handful of dry roasted peanuts
1 handful of fresh coriander/cilantro leaves, roughly chopped, to serve
sea salt and freshly ground black pepper
warm rotis or boiled rice, to serve

1 To make the spice mix, add the spices to a small frying pan and dry-fry for 30 seconds or so, stirring so they don't burn. The seeds should just start to colour. Remove from the heat, put in a blender and whiz to a powder.

2 To make the sauce, heat the oil in a large, heavy-based pan. Add the onion, season with salt and pepper and cook for 2–3 minutes until the onion begins to soften. Stir in the ginger, garlic, turmeric, garam masala and tamarind paste. Tip in the spice mix, tomatoes, coconut milk and chickpeas/ garbanzos and let the mixture bubble for a minute. Break up the tomatoes up with a wooden spoon, stir in the potatoes and cook with the lid on for about 15 minutes, or until the potatoes are fork tender. Top up with hot water from the kettle if the mixture begins to get too dry.

3 Stir in the peas and peanuts and cook for 5 minutes more. Taste and season some more if needed. Top with coriander/ cilantro leaves and serve with warm roti or rice if you wish. `

For non-vegans...
You could add some finely sliced beef for meat-eaters (see page 60).

Vegetable kebabs with miso & ginger glaze

The fresh figs add a delicious sweetness but they are not always available so use when in season. You've got licence to be as creative as you wish with the vegetables, but choose veg that take about the same time to cook and cut them into similar-sized pieces.

Serves 4
Prep: 30 mins Cook: 10 mins

1 aubergine/eggplant, cut into
    chunky pieces
2–3 courgettes/zucchini, cut into
    chunky pieces
4–6 figs, quartered
2 slices of sourdough bread, cubed
1 red pepper, deseeded and roughly
    chopped
1 green pepper, deseeded and
    roughly chopped
about 6 tomatoes, roughly chopped

FOR THE SLAW
½ light green cabbage, shredded
2 carrots, grated
juice of 1 lime
2 tbsp rice vinegar
2 shallots, finely chopped
1 red chilli, deseeded and finely
    chopped
1 garlic clove, finely chopped
2.5cm/1in piece of fresh root ginger,
    peeled and grated
a pinch of demerara/turbinado sugar,
    to taste
sea salt and freshly ground black
    pepper

FOR THE DRESSING
1 tbsp red miso paste
2 tbsp extra virgin olive oil
2.5cm/1in piece of fresh root ginger,
    peeled and grated

1 You will need 8 skewers. If you are using wooden skewers, soak them for 20 minutes before using – this will stop them from burning in the griddle pan.

2 First make the slaw. Put the cabbage and carrots in a large bowl, season with salt and pepper and mix together. In another bowl, whisk the lime juice, vinegar, shallots, chilli, garlic, ginger and sugar and whisk until the sugar dissolves. Pour the mixture into the cabbage and carrots and mix it all together using your hands. Leave to one side or in the refrigerator until ready to serve.

3 Now make the dressing. Mix the miso, oil and ginger together and season with salt and pepper.

4 Thread the aubergine/eggplant, courgette/zucchini, figs, bread, peppers and tomatoes evenly on to the skewers and lay them in a shallow dish. Drizzle the dressing over the top and turn to coat. Leave to one side for 10 minutes.

5 Heat a griddle pan until hot, then add the kebabs a few at a time. Cook for about 4–5 minutes each side, drizzling a little more dressing over them as they cook. Serve with the slaw and any leftover dressing on the side.

For non-vegans...
Cut 450g/1lb pork tenderloin into chunky cubes, and add to the skewers in between the vegetables. Cook for 6–8 minutes until the pork is tender and juicy.

Carrot & beetroot burger with red cabbage slaw

Making burgers from scratch is always preferable as you can decide exactly what goes into them – I like these with a bit of heat but adding the chilli flakes is up to you. Keep tasting the mixture in the pan until it is just right, then you know your burger will taste good!

Makes 8–10 burgers
Prep: 30 mins Cook: 20 mins

1 tbsp olive oil, plus extra for frying
1 onion, finely chopped
2 garlic cloves
1 tsp caraway seeds
1kg/2lb 4oz carrots, peeled and
   roughly grated
3 cooked beetroot/beet, grated
400g/14oz can of chickpeas/
   garbanzos or butter/lima beans,
   drained then chopped in food
   processor, juice reserved
a pinch of chilli flakes (optional)
1–2 tbsp plain/all-purpose flour, plus
   extra for dusting
sea salt and freshly ground black
   pepper
bread rolls, toasted, to serve

FOR THE SLAW
1 small red cabbage, shredded
300g/10½oz/1⅓ cups soy yogurt,
   plain or with almond
1 tbsp white wine vinegar
2 tsp Dijon mustard

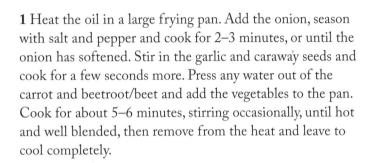

1 Heat the oil in a large frying pan. Add the onion, season with salt and pepper and cook for 2–3 minutes, or until the onion has softened. Stir in the garlic and caraway seeds and cook for a few seconds more. Press any water out of the carrot and beetroot/beet and add the vegetables to the pan. Cook for about 5–6 minutes, stirring occasionally, until hot and well blended, then remove from the heat and leave to cool completely.

2 Meanwhile, prepare the slaw. Put the cabbage in a large bowl. Mix together the yogurt, vinegar and mustard and season with salt and pepper. Spoon it over the cabbage and turn to coat. Leave to one side or in the refrigerator until ready to serve.

3 Line two baking/cookie sheets with parchment paper.

4 Add the chickpeas/garbanzos and chilli flakes, if using, to the carrot mixture and combine well, then pour in a little of the reserved juice to help bind the mixture. Spoon in the flour and stir to make quite a wet mixture. Scoop even-sized balls out with floured hands, flatten onto the prepared baking/cookie sheet into burgers and put in the refrigerator to chill.

5 When ready to cook, heat a little oil in a non-stick frying pan, add a few burgers at a time and cook for about 3–4 minutes on each side, or until golden and cooked through. Continue until all the burgers are cooked, adding more oil as you go.

6 Put some lettuce and tomato on each toasted roll, top with a burger and a dollop of slaw, finish with the top of the roll and serve.

For non-vegans...
Serve the burger with a slice of melted cheese on the top.

Pasta with fennel, pine nuts & pangrattato

Pangrattato simply means breadcrumbs in Italian and I think it makes the best storecupboard topping there is for pasta. This has a punchy mix of ingredients so there is no missing out on flavour.

Serves 4
Prep: 5 mins Cook: 20 mins

1 tbsp olive oil
½ red onion, finely chopped
2 garlic cloves, finely chopped
1 fennel bulb, trimmed and finely
    chopped, fronds reserved for
    garnish
a pinch of chilli flakes
4–6 sun-dried tomatoes, finely
    chopped
1 small handful of pine nuts
1 handful of basil leaves
350g/12oz linguine pasta
sea salt and freshly ground black
    pepper

FOR THE PANGRATTATO
1 tbsp olive oil
60g/2½oz/1 cup fine white
    breadcrumbs
1 garlic clove, grated
zest of ½ lemon
1 handful of flatleaf parsley leaves,
    finely chopped

1 First make the pangrattato. Heat the oil in a small frying pan. Add the breadcrumbs and cook for a minute or so, then stir in the garlic and lemon zest and cook briefly until the breadcrumbs start to turn golden. Stir in the parsley, season to taste and leave to one side.

2 Heat the olive oil in a large frying pan, add the onion and cook for 2–3 minutes until softened. Add the garlic, season well with salt and pepper and cook for 1 minute. Stir in the fennel, chilli flakes, sun-dried tomatoes and pine nuts and cook on low, stirring occasionally so it doesn't catch, for about 10 minutes until the fennel is just tender. Stir in the basil leaves and leave to one side.

3 Add the pasta to a large pan of just bubbling salted water and cook for about 10–12 minutes, or as per the pack instructions, until just tender. Drain and return to the pan with a little of the pasta water, then tip in the fennel mixture and turn to coat. Top with the pangrattato to serve.

For non-vegans...

Drain a 95g/3¼oz can of sardines in oil, then stir the fish into the fennel mixture along with a handful of cherry tomatoes and a few raisins to sweeten it and cut through the richness.

Spaghetti with sun-dried tomato pesto

I could eat this forever, it is such a classic combination. It is one of those dishes that always hits the spot and is a quick cook for when you are hungry. I like it with a lightly dressed rocket/arugula salad on the side. It's a good idea to double up the pesto – it will keep in the refrigerator for about a week and is great on roasted veggies.

Serves 4
Prep: 20 mins Cook: 15 mins

about 350g/12oz dried spaghetti
100g/3½oz /1 cup sun-dried
    tomatoes
2 garlic cloves
1 large handful of basil leaves
1 tbsp pine nuts
a pinch of chilli flakes
sea salt and freshly ground black
    pepper
about 4–5 tbsp extra virgin olive oil
rocket/arugula salad, lightly dressed,
    to serve

1 Put a large pan of salted water on to boil. Add the spaghetti and cook for about 10–12 minutes, or until cooked al dente. Drain and return to the pan with a little of the cooking water and toss to coat.

2 While the spaghetti is cooking, put the sun-dried tomatoes, garlic, basil, pine nuts, chilli flakes, salt and pepper and 1 tablespoon of oil in a food processor and whiz to blend, then trickle in the remaining oil and keep whizzing until the mixture is thick and well combined. Whiz it for longer if you prefer smooth pesto. Taste and season some more if needed.

3 Toss the hot spaghetti with the sauce and serve in shallow bowls with a sprinkling of black pepper and a lightly dressed rocket/arugula salad.

For non-vegans...
Add some freshly grated Parmesan to the pesto to taste, and scatter it over the prepared dish to serve.

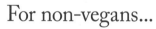

Sweet potato hash with chilli & preserved lemons

This is a great dish for using up leftover potatoes lurking in the vegetable basket or refrigerator. Swap your cabbage with the seasons – it works just as well in the winter with a Savoy or January King. A drizzle of pomegranate molasses adds the perfect sweetness and balances the flavours well, but it is not essential.

Serves 4
Prep: 15 mins Cook: 30 mins

4 sweet potatoes, peeled and cubed
1 light green cabbage (about
    700g/1lb 9oz), shredded
1–2 tbsp olive oil
4 spring onions/scallions, trimmed
    and finely chopped
2 garlic cloves, finely chopped
1 green chilli, deseeded and finely
    chopped
1 tsp mustard seeds
1 tsp ground cumin
2 preserved lemons, halved, pith
    removed and flesh chopped
1 handful of flatleaf parsley, leaves
    finely chopped
sea salt and freshly ground black
    pepper
a drizzle of pomegranate molasses,
    to serve (optional)

1 Put the sweet potatoes in pan of salted water and bring to the boil, then turn the heat down and simmer for 15 minutes, or until fork tender. Drain well and leave to one side to dry out a little.

2 Steam the cabbage in a steamer or put it in a colander with a pinch of salt, covered, over a pan of simmering water for about 5 minutes until tender but still with a bit of a bite to it. Remove and leave to one side.

3 Heat 1 tablespoon of the oil in a shallow, heavy-based pan. Add the spring onions/scallions, season with salt and pepper and cook for couple of minutes until softened. Stir in the garlic, chilli, mustard seeds and cumin and cook for a minute more, adding the remaining oil, if needed. Add the sweet potatoes, stirring and mashing lightly with a fork as you go, then tip in the cabbage and stir well to combine, making sure everything is coated in the flavoured oil. Cook for about 10 minutes, or until it starts to turn golden and a slight crust forms on the bottom. Stir in the preserved lemons and season some more if needed.

4 Scatter the parsley over the top and drizzle with the pomegranate molasses, if using, then serve straight from the pan.

For non-vegans...
Try adding some sliced chorizo to the pan along with the spring onions/scallions.

Bubble & squeak cakes with pickled beetroot

These moreish fritters are super-easy, and so good for using up weekend leftovers. I grate fresh horseradish into the potato when it is in season, otherwise use mustard or even wasabi. If you are using raw beetroot/beet, you'll need to roast it before pickling: roast at 180°C/350°F/Gas 4 for 1 hour, or until tender, then peel before use.

Serves 4–6 (makes about 10–12)
Prep: 20 mins Cook: 30 mins

1kg/2lb 4oz potatoes
2 tbsp sunflower spread
about 100ml/3½fl oz/scant ½ cup
   almond milk
½ Savoy cabbage, shredded
1–2 tsp Dijon mustard or a grating
   of fresh horseradish or wasabi
about 1–2 tbsp plain/all-purpose
   flour
olive oil, for cooking
sea salt and freshly ground black
   pepper

**FOR THE PICKLED BEETROOT/
BEET**

4 raw beetroots/beet, cooked (see
   above) or use ready cooked non-
   pickled beetroot/beet
2 tbsp rice vinegar
1–2 tsp caster/superfine sugar
1 star anise

For non-vegans...

Serve the cakes topped with a poached egg and some crisp bacon on the side, or try it with some crisply fried slices of black pudding or haggis.

1 Put the potatoes in a pan of salted water and bring to the boil, then turn the heat down and simmer for about 20 minutes, or until fork tender. Drain well, then return them to the pan and let them dry out a little. Add the sunflower spread and mash well, then add the milk and mash again until there are no lumps. Season well with salt and pepper.

2 While the potatoes are cooking, steam the cabbage in a steamer or in a colander, covered with a lid, over a pan of simmering water. Cook for about 5 minutes until just tender, then remove from the heat and leave to cool.

3 Mix the potato and cabbage together, then mix in the mustard or horseradish or wasabi and adjust the seasoning to taste. Scoop up a handful of the mixture and roll into a ball, then flatten into a patty. Repeat until you have used all the mixture to make about 12 patties. Tip the flour onto a plate and lightly coat each one. Put in the refrigerator to chill while you make the beetroot/beet.

4 Slice the cooked beetroot/beet and put it in a non-metallic bowl. Mix the vinegar with the sugar, season with salt and pepper, then pour this over the beetroot and add the star anise. Leave to one side for the flavours to mingle.

5 Heat a little oil in a non-stick frying pan, add a few cakes at a time and cook for about 2–3 minutes each side, or until golden and crisp, continuing until all the cakes are cooked, and adding a little more oil as you need it. Pile them high and serve with the beetroot/beet.

Roasted shiitake mushroom stroganoff

This is wonderfully rich and creamy. Roasting the mushrooms enriches their flavour and adds a wonderful 'meatiness' to the dish, while the courgette/zucchini gives it texture. This is good served with some fluffy white rice.

Serves 4
Prep: 15 mins Cook: 40 mins

250g/8oz shiitake mushrooms, large
   ones halved or quartered
8 portobello mushrooms, quartered
2 tbsp olive oil
1 onion, finely chopped
2 garlic cloves, finely chopped
1 tsp mustard seeds
a pinch of freshly grated nutmeg
2 tsp paprika
1 courgette/zucchini, grated
1 glass of white wine (about
   150ml/5fl oz/scant ⅔ cup)
1 tsp Dijon mustard
a few thyme stalks, leaves only
2 tsp cornflour/cornstarch
300ml/10½fl oz/1¼ cups
   almond milk
300ml/10½fl oz/1¼ cups
   mushroom or vegetable stock
1 handful of flatleaf parsley leaves,
   finely chopped
sea salt and freshly ground black
   pepper
boiled white rice, to serve

1 Preheat the oven to 200°C/400°F/Gas 6. Put all the mushrooms in a roasting pan, add half the olive oil, season with salt and pepper and toss together. Roast for 20 minutes. Remove and leave to one side.

2 Heat the remaining oil over a medium heat in a large frying pan. Add the onion, season with salt and pepper and cook for 2–3 minutes until beginning to soften. Stir in the garlic and cook for few seconds more. Stir in the mustard seeds, nutmeg and paprika, then stir in the courgette/zucchini and cook for 5 minutes until pale golden. Raise the heat, add the wine and let it bubble for 1–2 minutes, then reduce to a simmer and stir in the mustard and thyme. Mix the cornflour/cornstarch with the almond milk, then pour it into the pan, stirring continuously, and add the stock. Bring to the boil, then turn the heat down and simmer about 10 minutes, or until the sauce is thickened.

3 Tip in the roasted mushrooms and stir gently to coat them in the sauce. Stir in half the parsley, spoon into shallow bowls and sprinkle over the remaining parsley. Serve with fluffy white rice.

For non-vegans...
Cut a pork tenderloin into bite-sized pieces and pan-fry until cooked through and no longer pink, then stir it into the dish. A spoonful of cream could also be stirred in at the end.

Tofu, broad bean, lemon & garlic stir-fry

A quick home-from-work dish that is packed with flavours – it's a bit of a fusion between Chinese and Thai cusines and tastes incredibly fresh. The lemon slices and radish add colour and crunch. It is up to you whether you peel the broad/fava beans but, if you are not going to peel them, you might want to use fewer of them in the dish.

Serves 4
Prep: 15 mins Cook: 20 mins

about 3–4 tbsp toasted sesame oil
300g/10½oz/2½ cups firm tofu, cut
    into bite-sized cubes
1 bunch of spring onions/scallions,
    trimmed and sliced on the
    diagonal
4 garlic cloves, finely sliced into
    slivers
5cm/1¾in piece of fresh root ginger,
    peeled and finely sliced into
    slivers
½ lemongrass stalk, finely chopped
1 Chinese nappa cabbage, or use
    light green cabbage, trimmed and
    finely shredded
300g/10½oz/2½ cups frozen broad/
    fava beans, defrosted
1 tbsp dark soy sauce
1 tbsp mirin
1 tbsp rice vinegar
juice of ½ lemon
sea salt and freshly ground black
    pepper
1 large lemon, skin and pith
    removed, flesh sliced into fine
    rounds
4–5 radishes, finely sliced
2 tsp black sesame seeds
1 handful of Thai basil leaves

1 Heat a little of the oil in a wok, add the tofu pieces a few at a time and fry for about 5–6 minutes until golden, turning half way through. Remove from the heat and transfer to a plate lined with paper towels. Continue cooking the remaining tofu, adding more oil as needed.

2 Add a tiny amount of oil to the pan, add the spring onions/scallions and season with salt and pepper. Cook on high, moving them around the pan, for 1–2 minutes until beginning to soften, then add the garlic, ginger and lemongrass and continue cooking for a couple of minutes more, being careful not to burn the garlic. Now add the cabbage and toss with the spices, then add the broad/fava beans and turn to mix everything together.

3 Mix together the soy sauce, mirin, rice vinegar and lemon juice. Push the cabbage mix to one side of the pan and add the soy sauce mixture, letting it bubble for a minute or so, then stir-fry to incorporate everything together.

4 Remove from the heat, tip in the tofu and lemon pieces and stir. Scatter over the radish slices, black sesame seeds and top with Thai basil to serve.

For non-vegans...

Chicken is the obvious addition if you want to add some meat. Either poach chicken breasts in hot vegetable stock for about 20 minutes until tender and cooked through, or add the chicken to the sesame oil instead of the tofu and fry until cooked through.

Butter bean & courgette cakes with cucumber relish

This is packed with yummy flavours. The mix does seem a little wet but once in the pan and left to cook until crisp and golden, the patties will hold together. The pepper was a last-minute addition, and adds an element of crunch and a pleasing fleck of colour. This is much easier if you use a non-stick pan.

Makes 10–12
Prep: 15 mins Cook: 15 mins

1 tbsp olive oil, plus extra for frying
2 large courgettes/zucchini, grated
    and squeezed to remove the
    water
a pinch of freshly grated nutmeg
zest of 1 lemon
a pinch of chilli flakes
400g/14oz can of butter/lima beans,
    drained and juice reserved
3 spring onions/scallions, trimmed
    and roughly chopped
2 garlic cloves, roughly chopped
1 red pepper, deseeded and roughly
    chopped
2 tsp sesame seeds
1 tbsp plain/all-purpose flour
about 1–2 tbsp olive oil
sea salt and freshly ground black
    pepper
a few basil leaves to garnish
    (optional)
1 large handful of watercress, to
    serve

FOR THE CUCUMBER RELISH
½ cucumber, halved lengthways,
    seeds removed and cut into half
    moon shapes
1 tbsp rice vinegar

1 Heat the oil in a large frying pan. Add the courgettes/zucchini, nutmeg, lemon zest and chilli flakes, season and cook for a few minutes, stirring occasionally so it doesn't catch and burn. Remove the pan from the heat.

2 Put the butter/lima beans, spring onions/scallions, garlic, pepper and sesame seeds in a food processor and pulse until well mixed but still with some texture. Pour away any water in the pan from the courgettes/zucchini, then add the bean mixture and slowly fold in the flour. Put it in the refrigerator while you prepare the cucumber.

3 Mix the cucumber, rice vinegar and a pinch of salt in a bowl. Taste and season some more if needed. Set aside.

4 Heat a drizzle of oil in a non-stick frying pan, add a tablespoonful of the mix and pat it down using a spatula or fish slice to form a cake shape. Leave to cook undisturbed for about 5 minutes, or until the underside is golden, crisp and firm enough to turn over. Cook the other side for about the same time, then remove from the pan. Continue cooking until you have used all the mixture, adding oil as needed.

5 Garnish with basil leaves, if using, and watercress, then serve with the cucumber relish.

For non-vegans...
Whiz a few cooked prawns into the mixture to make a cheat's fishcake for any non-vegan diners.

Cottage pie topped with potato & parsnip mash

This will certainly hit the spot and satisfy on a cold day. Using a mushroom stock really enriches the 'gravy' and gives it the umami kick. Make sure you really caramelize the diced carrots and parsnips – you'll reap the benefits with flavour.

Serves 4
Prep: 15 mins Cook: 1 hour

1 tbsp olive oil
1 onion, finely chopped
2 garlic cloves, finely chopped
3 carrots, diced
1 parsnip, peeled and diced
200g/7oz/heaped 1 cup dried Puy
    lentils, rinsed
1 bay leaf (optional)
a few rosemary stalks, leaves finely
    chopped (optional)
a pinch of freshly grated nutmeg
a pinch of ground cinnamon
1 tbsp tomato purée/paste
1 glass of red wine (about 150ml/
    5fl oz/scant ⅔ cup)
a splash of tamari or dark soy sauce
about 500ml/17fl oz/generous
    2 cups hot mushroom or
    vegetable stock
sea salt and freshly ground black
    pepper
steamed greens, to serve

FOR THE TOPPING
900g/2lb potatoes, peeled and
    quartered
3 parsnips, peeled and roughly
    chopped
2 tbsp olive oil spread, margarine or
    dairy-free spread of your choice,
    plus extra for topping
about 200ml/7fl oz/scant 1 cup
    unsweetened almond milk or
    dairy-free milk of your choice

1 Heat the oil in a large, heavy-based pan. Add the onion, season with salt and pepper and cook on a low to medium heat, stirring occasionally, for 2–3 minutes until softened. Add the garlic and cook for a minute more, being careful not to burn the garlic. Now add the carrots and parsnip, add a drizzle more oil if needed, turn the heat up a little and cook for 6–8 minutes until just starting to turn golden, stirring so they don't burn. Add the lentils, turning so they soak up all the juices.

2 Add the bay, the rosemary, if using, and the nutmeg and cinnamon and stir well, then stir in the tomato purée/paste and wine, raise the heat and let it bubble for a couple of minutes. Add the tamari and stock, give it a final stir, then put the lid on and let it simmer away for about 30 minutes, or until the lentils are softened and a lot of the liquid has been absorbed. If it starts to dry out too much, top up with a little hot water from the kettle but be aware that the more you add, the more you are diluting the flavour.

3 Preheat the oven to 200°C/400°F/Gas 6.

4 While the lentils are cooking, make the topping. Put the potatoes and parsnips in a pan of salted water and bring to the boil. Turn the heat down and simmer for 15–20 minutes until the potatoes are fork tender. Drain well, then return to pan. Add the olive oil spread or margarine and mash well until there are no lumps, then pour in the almond milk and mash again until creamy.

5 Ladle the lentil mixture and all the sauce into an ovenproof dish, then spoon the mash over and even out with a fork. Dot with margarine and bake for 25 minutes, until bubbling and piping hot. Serve alone or with some delicious greens.

Sweet, hot & sour squash & mushroom one-pan

This isn't sweet and sour as you know it, but it has all the elements without the over-rich sauce. Shiitake mushrooms add a great earthiness to the dish but it's good with button or chestnut/cremini mushrooms too. I like this with fluffy white rice as it soaks up all the delicious juices, but brown would also work if you prefer.

Serves 4
Prep: 15 mins Cook: 30 mins

1 tbsp olive oil
1 red onion, roughly chopped
1 red chilli, sliced lengthways, deseeded and sliced into fine fingers
2 garlic cloves, finely sliced into slivers
a pinch of sumac
1 butternut squash, peeled, halved, deseeded and cut into bite-sized pieces
2 sage leaves, finely chopped
200ml/7fl oz/scant 1 cup hot vegetable stock
200g/7oz shiitake mushrooms, larger ones quartered
1 tbsp red wine vinegar
2 tsp sugar
1 large handful of mint leaves, finely chopped
sea salt and freshly ground black pepper
cooked rice, to serve

1 Heat the oil in a large shallow, heavy-based pan. Add the onion, season with salt and pepper and cook for 2–3 minutes until softened. Add the chilli and garlic and cook for a few seconds more, then stir in the sumac, squash and sage leaves. Cook on a fairly high heat for about 6–8 minutes, until the squash is starting to turn pale golden, stirring continuously so it doesn't catch.

2 Raise the heat to high and pour in the stock, bubble for a few minutes, then turn the heat down and simmer with the lid on for 15 minutes, or until the squash is tender. Add the mushrooms, give it a stir and sit the lid back on. There should still be some liquid but if it is drying out too much, top up with a little hot water from the kettle, but you don't want it swimming in it (it isn't a casserole). Cook for few minutes to soften the mushrooms.

3 Remove from the heat and let it stand for 5 minutes, adjusting the seasoning to taste. Mix together the vinegar and sugar and pour the mixture into the pan, then add the mint and gently stir it all together so you don't break up the squash. Serve with rice of your choice.

For non-vegans...
Fry up some slices of pork or chicken until tender and cooked through, then add them to the pan with the squash.

Squash & chicory rosti

When making this dish, I like to parboil the squash and potato first before grating them. I can then feel happier in the knowledge that it is going to be fully cooked once in the frying pan – I am not sure this is the authentic way to make a rosti, but then adding squash and chicory is hardly very Swiss. It is much easier to turn these rosti if you use a non-stick pan.

Serves 4 (makes 4 x 21cm/8¼in rostis)
Prep: 15 mins   Cook: 30 mins

4 waxy potatoes, peeled
1 large butternut squash, halved, deseeded, peeled and cut into large chunky pieces
4 heads of chicory/Belgian endive, grated
about 2–4 tbsp sunflower spread
sea salt and freshly ground black pepper
gherkins, sliced, to serve

1 Put the potatoes in a large pan of salted water and bring to the boil, then turn the heat down and simmer for about 5 minutes. Add the squash and cook for about 8–10 minutes, or until both potatoes and squash are just tender. Don't let them over-cook and become too soft. Drain well and leave to one side to cool.

2 Once cool, grate the potatoes and squash into a large bowl. Add the chicory/Belgian endive, season really well with salt and pepper and stir carefully to combine.

3 Heat a quarter of the sunflower spread in a small non-stick frying pan, spoon in a quarter of the rosti mixture and pat it down to fill the pan. Cook over a medium heat for about 5–6 minutes, or until the underside is golden and crisp. Remove from the heat and transfer to a plate, continue to cook the remaining rostis in the same way. To serve, slice and serve with gherkins.

For non-vegans...
Serve each rosti with a poached egg on top, or a scattering of goats' cheese.

Almost paella

This is sweet and fragrant, thanks to the saffron, paprika and sherry. It is one of those dishes that tastes good straight from the pot or reheated the next day. Swap the broad/fava beans for peas, if you prefer. When looking for vegan sherry, follow the same rules as you would for wine (see page 15).

Serves 4
Prep: 15 mins Cook: 25 mins

1 tbsp olive oil
1 onion, finely chopped
2 garlic cloves, finely chopped
2 red peppers, deseeded and finely
    diced
a pinch of saffron strands
2 tsp sweet mild paprika
200g/7oz/heaped 1 cup basmati
    rice
200ml/7fl oz/scant 1 cup vegan
    sherry or white wine
500ml/17fl oz/generous 2 cups hot
    vegetable stock
a few thyme stalks
100g/3½oz/scant ¾ cup frozen
    sweetcorn kernels, defrosted
    and soaked in boiling water for
    4 minutes then drained
100g/3½oz/heaped ¾ cup frozen
    broad/fava beans, defrosted
    and soaked in boiling water for
    4 minutes, then drained and
    peeled if you wish
10 cherry tomatoes, halved
1 handful of flatleaf parsley leaves,
    finely chopped
sea salt and freshly ground black
    pepper
lemon wedges, to serve

1 Heat the oil in a large, shallow pan. Add the onion, season with salt and pepper and cook for 2–3 minutes until beginning to soften. Stir in the garlic and cook for a few seconds, then add the peppers and cook for 2–3 minutes, stirring occasionally and being careful that the garlic doesn't burn.

2 Stir in the saffron and paprika and cook for a few seconds, then stir in the rice until it is all coated in the spices and flavourings. Raise the heat and add the sherry or wine and let it bubble for a minute or so. Pour in the stock, keep it bubbling a little longer, then turn the heat down to a simmer and cook for about 20 minutes until rice is almost tender and has absorbed a lot of the liquid.

3 Add the thyme leaves, sweetcorn, broad/fava beans and tomatoes, and stir it really well so everything is blended. Taste and season some more if needed. Scatter the parsley over the top and serve with lemon wedges.

For non-vegans...

Add some chopped cooking chorizo to the pan with the onion at the start of cooking. Top the finished dish some large shell-on cooked prawns/shrimp to make this a more traditional paella.

Peking pancakes with pickled cucumber

This recipe contains the same punchy Asian flavours as traditional Peking duck pancakes and the cucumber adds the perfect crunch. The pancake mix sets very quickly so it might take a few tries to get a perfect round. Whatever shape they are, they will be delicious!

Serves 4
Prep: 15 mins Cook: 30 mins

1 tbsp rice vinegar
½ cucumber, halved lengthways, seeds removed and cut into sticks
1–2 aubergines/eggplants, roughly chopped
2 tsp Chinese five-spice
2 tsp maple syrup
about 2 tbsp olive oil
1 handful of chestnut/cremini mushrooms, finely sliced
a splash of dark soy sauce
2 spring onions/scallions, trimmed and finely sliced lengthways
sea salt and freshly ground black pepper

FOR THE PANCAKES
250g/9oz/1⅔ cups rice flour
2 tbsp cornflour/cornstarch
a pinch of Chinese five-spice
800ml/28 fl oz/scant 3½ cups soy milk
½ tbsp toasted sesame oil

TO SERVE
plum or sriracha sauce
a few coriander/cilantro leaves

For non-vegans...
Add some cooked shredded duck or sliced steak to the pancake filling.

1 First make the pancakes. Put the rice flour and cornflour/cornstarch in a bowl, add a pinch of salt and the five-spice, then pour in the soy milk and whisk until smooth. Top up with about 2 tablespoons of water or non-dairy milk and whisk again if the batter is too thick.

2 Heat a tiny amount of toasted sesame oil and swirl it around a crêpe pan or small, flat, non-stick frying pan until it just coats. When very hot, add a small ladleful of the batter and, moving quickly, tip the pan so the batter coats as much of the pan as it can. Loosen the edges with a round-ended knife and as soon as the underside is ready, which will take seconds, flip it over using a fish slice. Cook for a further few seconds, then transfer it to an upturned plate. Layer the pancakes between parchment paper as you cook the rest.

3 Put the rice vinegar in a bowl and add the cucumber sticks and a pinch of salt. Leave to one side.

4 To make the filling, toss the aubergine/eggplant with the five-spice, maple syrup and a drizzle of oil and season with salt and pepper. Heat a little of the oil in a large frying pan and add the aubergine/eggplant and cook over a fairly high heat for about 10 minutes until tender and starting to turn golden. Push the aubergine/eggplant to one side, add the mushrooms and soy sauce and cook for 2–3 minutes, moving them around the pan.

5 To assemble, lay the pancakes out, spoon some aubergine/eggplant and mushrooms down the middle, top with cucumber and spring onion and roll up. Slice in half on the diagonal and dig in! If you have a favourite sauce, plum or sriracha maybe, add a drizzle of this to the roll or serve on the side if you wish.

4

FOOD TO SHARE

Courgette, dill & tomato tart

A thin layer of mustard over the base of the pastry shell adds a fantastic tang to this tart. Without the usual custard base of a quiche, the full flavour of the tomatoes and courgettes/ zucchini really shines through, making this a delightfully fresh addition to any table.

Serves 6
Prep: 15 mins Cook: 45 mins

1 tbsp olive oil
½ red onion, finely chopped
2 garlic cloves, finely chopped
2–3 small courgettes/zucchini, finely
   sliced
a pinch of dried oregano
a few stalks of dill, finely chopped,
   plus extra for topping
2 tsp Dijon mustard
4–5 tomatoes, sliced widthways into
   1cm/¾in slices
a few pitted black olives (optional)
a drizzle of extra virgin olive oil
a drizzle of balsamic vinegar
sea salt and freshly ground black
   pepper
a lightly dressed salad, to serve

FOR THE PASTRY
225g/8oz/1¾ cups plain/all-purpose
   flour, sifted, plus extra for dusting
a pinch of salt
125g/4oz sunflower spread

1 To make the pastry, mix the flour and a pinch of salt in a large bowl. Add the sunflower spread and rub in until it looks like breadcrumbs, then add 2 teaspoons of ice cold water and bring together to form a dough. Turn out onto a floured board and form into a ball, wrap with cling film/plastic wrap and put it in the refrigerator to rest for 20 minutes.

2 Preheat the oven to 200°C/400°F/Gas 6 and grease a 20cm/8in tart pan.

3 Heat the oil in a frying pan. Add the onion, season and cook for 2–3 minutes until beginning to soften. Stir in the garlic and cook for a few seconds more. Add the courgettes/ zucchini, oregano and dill and cook on low, stirring occasionally, for 2–3 minutes, until just golden. Set aside.

4 Remove the pastry from the refrigerator, sit it on a lightly floured surface and roll out to a circle slightly larger than the pan. Lay the pastry over the tin with the edges overlapping. Fill with parchment paper and baking beans and bake for 15 minutes, or until the edges of the pastry are just beginning to turn pale golden. Remove from the oven, remove the beans and paper, smear the base with the mustard, then put it back in the oven for couple more minutes until crisp. Remove from the oven, trim the pastry edges and leave to cool. Turn the oven down to 190°C/375°F/Gas 5.

5 Fill the pastry case with alternating slices of courgette/ zucchini and tomato, top with tomato slices and scatter the olives over the top, if using, then drizzle over the oil and balsamic vinegar and bake for 20–30 minutes until golden.

6 Leave to rest for 5–10 minutes at least before slicing. Serve hot or at room temperature, scattered with dill and with a lightly dressed salad alongside.

For non-vegans...
Layer a few canned anchovies between the vegetables for little pockets of salty flavour.

Chickpea & pine nut balls in hot tomato sauce

This is rather like eating a good nut roast in a rich tomato sauce. I serve these with cubed rosemary potatoes in winter, or rice and a rocket/arugula salad in the warmer months.

Serves 4 (makes 20 small balls)
Prep: 20 mins Cook: 50 mins

1 tbsp olive oil
1 red onion, very finely chopped
2 garlic cloves, grated
1 tsp sumac
2 tomatoes
40g/1½oz/heaped ¼ cup pine nuts
400g/14oz can of chickpeas/
    garbanzos, drained, juice
    reserved to use in baking (see
    page 16)
5–6 tbsp fine breadcrumbs
zest and juice of 1 small lemon
1 tsp tahini
a few thyme sprigs, leaves only
1 handful of flatleaf parsley leaves,
    finely chopped
sea salt and freshly ground black
    pepper

FOR THE SAUCE
1 tbsp olive oil
1 onion, finely chopped
2 garlic cloves, finely chopped
1 red chilli, deseeded and finely
    chopped
a pinch of dried oregano
600g/1lb 5oz jar of passata/sieved
    tomatoes
a pinch of chilli flakes

TO SERVE
roasted rosemary potatoes, brown
    rice or a rocket/arugula salad

1 To make the balls, heat the oil in a frying pan, add the red onion and cook for 1–2 minutes. Add the garlic and sumac and cook until translucent, around 2 minutes. Set aside.

2 To skin the tomatoes, cut a cross on the base of each one and place in a bowl. Pour boiling water over and leave for 30 seconds, then plunge into cold water and peel away the skin.

3 Put the pine nuts, chickpeas/garbanzos and breadcrumbs in a food processor and pulse until chopped. Add the tomatoes, lemon zest and juice, tahini, thyme leaves and parsley and pulse again until combined but retaining some texture. Add the cooked onion, season to taste and pulse again.

4 With wet hands, roll into 20 balls. Line a baking sheet with parchment paper, arrange the balls on the sheet and put in the refrigerator to chill while you make the sauce.

5 Preheat the oven to 200°C/400°F/Gas 6.

6 To make the sauce, heat the oil in a deep frying pan. Add the onion, season and cook for 2–3 minutes until soft. Stir in the garlic, chilli and oregano and cook for a minute more. Pour in the passata/sieved tomatoes, fill the jar with water and add to the pan. Bring to the boil, then reduce to a simmer, stir in the chilli flakes and cook for 20 minutes more, topping up with hot water if it starts to thicken too much.

7 Meanwhile, put the balls in a roasting pan and roast for about 25 minutes, or until golden.

8 To serve, add the balls to the sauce and take straight to the table so everyone can help themselves. Serve with cubed roast rosemary potatoes, brown rice or a lightly dressed salad of rocket/arugula leaves.

Caramelized leek risotto

This recipe started life as leek and wild garlic risotto. Wild garlic is delicious but it's a shame it only has a short growing season, in late spring. If it is the right time of year and you can pick some, chop it into the risotto. Get the leeks nice and golden and tinged brown as this is where all the flavour comes from – the zing of lemon and fresh basil cut through the richness.

Serves 4
Prep: 15 mins Cook: 40 mins

1 tbsp olive oil
125g/4oz sunflower spread
5 shallots, finely chopped
3 garlic cloves, finely chopped
3 leeks, trimmed, washed and finely
    sliced
zest of 1 lemon
a pinch of chilli flakes
300g/10½oz/1⅔ cups arborio
    risotto rice
1 glass of white wine
750ml/26fl oz/3 cups hot vegetable
    stock
1 handful of fresh basil leaves, torn,
    plus extra to garnish
sea salt and freshly ground black
    pepper

1 Heat the olive oil and sunflower spread in a large, deep frying pan. Add the shallots, season with salt and pepper and cook for 2–3 minutes until beginning to soften. Stir in the garlic and cook for a minute more. Add the leeks, half the lemon zest and the chilli flakes and cook on a fairly high heat for about 8–10 minutes until golden and caramelized. Stir in the rice, making sure the grains get coated.

2 Pour in the wine, raise the heat a little, stir and cook for a couple of minutes. Add about half the stock and turn the heat down to a simmer. Keep stirring and gradually adding the stock until the rice is just tender, about 15–20 minutes. It should be fairly wet in consistency. Adjust the seasoning to taste with salt, pepper and chilli. Add the lemon zest and basil and stir it through to serve with a few extra basil leaves on top.

For non-vegans...
Crumble some Stilton or Parmesan cheese over the top of the risotto, and leave to melt for a couple of minutes to melt in.

Purple sprouting broccoli & mushroom lasagne

Lasagne is often seen as a midweek meal but in fact it is quite a time-consuming dish to make with lots of components. It is certainly a good one to make ahead as it often tastes even better reheated. A lasagne should be lots of thin layers, not sloppy and loose, and you should be able to cut it into even squares that remain stacked. For an even richer lasagne, you could use the ragu from Mushroom Ragu with Home-Made Tagliatelle (see page 110).

Serves 4–6
Prep: 30 mins Cook: 1½ hours

FOR THE RAGU
2 tbsp olive oil
1 onion, finely chopped
2 garlic cloves, finely chopped
2 celery stalks, finely chopped
2 carrots, finely chopped
400g/14oz can of plum tomatoes, chopped
400g/14oz chestnut/cremini mushrooms, finely chopped
220g/7¼oz purple sprouting broccoli or use Tenderstem or regular broccoli, trimmed
about 16–18 sheets of egg-free lasagne
1 handful of fine breadcrumbs, for topping
sea salt and freshly ground black pepper

continued opposite

1 First make the ragu. Heat half the oil in a large, heavy-based pan. Add the onion, season with salt and pepper and cook for 2–3 minutes until beginning to soften. Stir in the garlic and cook for a minute more. Add the celery and carrot and cook over a low heat for about another 10 minutes or so, adding a little more oil if needed. Pour in the tomatoes and 500ml/17fl oz/generous 2 cups of hot water from the kettle, breaking up the tomatoes with a wooden spoon. Bring to the boil, then turn the heat down and simmer with the lid partially on for about 1 hour, topping up with more hot water if needed, but it shouldn't be swimming in liquid.

2 Meanwhile, heat the remaining oil in a frying pan. Add the mushrooms, season with salt and pepper, and cook for 3 minutes until just starting to brown. Remove from the heat and put to one side.

3 Preheat the oven to 200°C/400°F/Gas 6 and have a 26cm/10½in long ovenproof dish ready.

4 Bring a large pan of salted water to the boil, add the broccoli and cook for 5–6 minutes, or until just soft. Drain well.

5 I always pre-cook the lasagne sheets even if the pack says it's not necessary as it is easier to layer and you can be assured that it will be cooked and tender. Bring a large pan of

FOR THE BÉCHAMEL
150g/5oz sunflower spread
1½ tbsp cornflour/cornstarch
about 700ml/24fl oz/3 cups almond
    milk or soy milk
a generous pinch of freshly grated
    nutmeg
sea salt and freshly ground black
    pepper

TO SERVE
rocket/arugula salad

water to the boil, add the sheets and boil for a few minutes until soft, then drain and separate the sheets so they are ready to use.

6 To make the béchamel sauce, heat the sunflower spread in a pan, stir in the flour using a wooden spoon, then trickle in a little almond milk, stirring and adding more milk until smooth. It might be easier to switch to a balloon whisk to prevent any lumps forming. Add nutmeg to taste and season well with salt and pepper.

7 To assemble, smear a little of the béchamel on the base of the dish then layer up about four or five layers of ragu, lasagne, béchamel, broccoli and mushrooms, adding just a little each time. Finish with enough sauce to smooth out over the top, then sprinkle over the breadcrumbs. Bake for about 35–45 minutes, or until golden and bubbling. Leave to stand for 5 minutes before slicing to serve. Serve with a lightly dressed rocket/arugula salad.

For non-vegans...
Add a layer of roughly chopped hard-boiled eggs between the lasagne sheets and the broccoli as you build the lasagne.

Vegetable makhani

This curry recipe isn't about being hot, it is made mild and creamy by the cashew nuts and almond milk.

Serves 4
Prep: 20 mins Cook: 40 mins

1 cauliflower, broken into florets
300g/10½oz fine green beans,
    trimmed
4 large potatoes, peeled and cut into
    bite-sized pieces
1 tbsp olive oil or sunflower spread
1 onion, finely chopped
1 red chilli, halved and deseeded
5cm/1¾in piece of fresh root ginger,
    peeled and roughly chopped
2 garlic cloves, roughly chopped
1 tbsp garam masala
2 tsp ground fenugreek
seeds from 4 cardamom pods,
    crushed
a pinch of curry leaves, crushed
    between the fingers
1 tbsp tomato purée/paste
6 tomatoes, whizzed in the food
    processor
150g/5oz/1½ cups cashew nuts,
    ground
1 tbsp maple syrup
200ml/7fl oz/scant 1 cup almond
    milk or soy milk
1 cinnamon stick
a few coriander/cilantro leaves, to
    garnish
sea salt and freshly ground black
    pepper
boiled rice, to serve

1 Steam the cauliflower and green beans until just tender and leave to one side. Put the potatoes in a pan of salted water and bring to the boil, then turn the heat down and simmer for about 15 minutes, or until fork tender. Drain well and leave to one side.

2 Heat the oil in a large, heavy-based pan. Add the onion, season with salt and pepper and cook for 2–3 minutes until softened. Stir in the chilli, ginger and garlic and cook for a few minutes more. Stir in the garam masala, fenugreek, cardamom seeds and curry leaves and cook for a further few seconds. Add the tomato purée/paste and tomatoes and turn to coat. Bring to the boil, then add the cashew nuts and maple syrup and simmer gently for about 10–15 minutes, topping up with hot water from the kettle if needed. Pour the mixture into a food processor and blitz until smooth, then pour in the almond or soy milk and whiz again. Pour it all back into the pan and simmer gently until hot, adjusting the seasoning to taste.

3 Add the potatoes, green beans and cauliflower and give it a stir so it is all coated. Continue simmering gently to warm the vegetables through, topping up with hot water from the kettle if needed. Transfer to shallow bowls, garnish with coriander/cilantro leaves and serve with rice.

Cauliflower & bean biryani with crisp onions

This can be time-consuming as it has a few stages so it is worth making a larger quantity to serve when there is a bit of a gathering – any leftovers are good too.

Serves 6–8
Prep: 15 mins Cook: 1½ hours

500g/1lb 2oz/2¾ cups white
    basmati rice
1 bay leaf
about 6 cardamom pods, crushed
2 tbsp olive oil
2 onions, roughly chopped
2 garlic cloves, finely chopped
5cm/1¾in piece of fresh root ginger,
    peeled and finely sliced
1 red chilli, deseeded and finely
    chopped
1 tbsp garam masala
2 tsp ground turmeric
300g/10½oz fine green beans,
    trimmed and chopped into
    3 pieces
1 medium cauliflower, cut into
    florets
500g/1lb 4oz/2 cups soy yogurt
125g/4oz sunflower spread
a pinch of saffron strands
1 handful of coriander/cilantro
    leaves, finely chopped (plus extra
    for topping)
1 handful of mint leaves, finely
    chopped
1 handful of flaked/slivered almonds,
    lightly toasted
hot pickle, to serve

FOR THE CRISP ONIONS
1–2 tbsp olive oil
3 onions, finely sliced into half
    moons

1 First cook the rice. Put the rice, bay leaf and cardamom into a pan, add a pinch of salt and cover with double the amount of water. Put the lid on and cook for 15 minutes, or until the rice is tender and the water has been absorbed. Remove from the heat and leave to one side with the lid on. Fluff up the rice with a fork when it has cooled slightly.

2 To make the crisp onions, heat the oil in a large frying pan, add the onions, season with salt and pepper and cook on a fairly high heat, stirring occasionally so they don't burn. Cook for about 20 minutes until caramelized and beginning to go crisp. Remove and leave to one side.

3 Meanwhile, heat the oil in a large, deep heavy-based pan (a casserole pot/Dutch oven is good). Add the onion, season with salt and pepper and cook for 2–3 minutes until softened. Stir in the garlic, ginger, chilli, garam masala and turmeric and cook for a few seconds. Add the green beans and cauliflower florets, then stir in the soy yogurt and 500ml/17fl oz/generous 2 cups hot water from the kettle. Simmer gently for about 15–20 minutes, or until the cauliflower and beans are tender. Remove from the heat and leave to cool a little, then transfer it to a large bowl.

4 Melt the sunflower spread, stir in the saffron and leave to one side. Preheat the oven to 190°C/375°F/Gas 5.

5 In your heavy casserole pot, spoon in a little rice, then layer up with the cauliflower mixture, a drizzle of saffron spread, the coriander/cilantro, mint and finish with rice and a sprinkling of almonds. Put the lid on and put it in the oven for about 15–20 minutes, or until the rice has a bit of a crust on it.

6 To serve, scatter over the crisp onions and remaining coriander/cilantro and serve with hot pickle.

Barley, mushroom & kale risotto with barberries

I think pearl barley works a treat in risottos. It may even be nicer than rice as the little pearls really absorb the flavour.

Serves 4
Prep: 15 mins, plus soaking
Cook: 30 mins

2 tbsp sunflower spread
2 tbsp olive oil
1 onion, finely chopped
2 garlic cloves, finely chopped
zest of 1 lemon
a few thyme leaves
200g/7oz/heaped 1 cup pearl barely
1 glass of white wine (about
    150ml/5fl oz/scant ⅔ cup)
20g/1oz/¾ cup dried porcini
    mushrooms (soaked in hot water
    for 10 minutes, drained and
    chopped, reserving the juice)
900ml/31fl oz/3⅔ cups hot
    vegetable stock
300g/10½oz chestnut/cremini
    mushrooms, sliced
1 large handful of kale, steamed
1 handful of dried barberries
    (optional)
1 handful of hazelnuts, toasted and
    chopped
sea salt and freshly ground black
    pepper

1 Heat sunflower spread and half the oil in a large frying pan. Add the onion, season with salt and pepper and cook for 2–3 minutes. Stir in the garlic, lemon zest and thyme and cook for a minute or so. Stir in in the pearl barley, making sure it soaks up all the juices. Raise the heat, pour in the wine and bubble for a minute, then add the drained porcini mushrooms and the stock. Strain and add the juice from the dried mushrooms. Stir well and cook on a low simmer for about 25 minutes, or until the pearl barley is tender, topping up with more hot water from the kettle if needed.

2 While this is cooking, add the remaining oil to a small frying pan and add the mushrooms. Cook for a few minutes, or until they begin to release their juices, then remove from the heat. Stir the kale and mushrooms into the risotto. Taste and season some more if needed, then scatter over the barberries, if using, and hazelnuts to serve.

For non-vegans...

Pearl barley absorbs plenty of flavour, so works well with chorizo. Stir in some cubes of cooking chorizo to the frying pan with the mushrooms, and be sure to pour the oils it releases into the risotto too.

Lentil & ale pie

Pies are real cold-weather food, hearty and filling. Lentils and aduki beans make a fabulous meat-free filling and chunky carrots and potatoes impart flavour and add texture. Bubbling away in ale and cooked under a crisp pastry crust - what could be better? Though most ales are vegan-friendly, it's always worth checking the label before cooking (or drinking!).

Serves 4
Prep: 30 mins Cook: 1½ hours

2 tbsp olive oil
1 handful of baby onions, peeled
2 garlic cloves, finely chopped
1 bay leaf
1 rosemary stalk, leaves finely
   chopped
300g/10½oz/1⅔ cups dried Puy
   lentils, rinsed
400g/14oz can of aduki beans,
   drained
4 carrots, roughly chopped
400ml/14fl oz/generous 1½ cups
   dark vegan ale
400ml/14fl oz/generous 1½ cups
   hot vegetable stock
2 tsp grainy mustard
4 potatoes, cooked and cut into
   chunky pieces
sea salt and freshly ground black
   pepper
steamed savoy cabbage or kale, to
   serve

FOR THE PASTRY
225g/8oz/heaped1¾ cups plain/
   all-purpose flour, sifted, plus extra
   for dusting
125g/4oz sunflower spread
almond milk, to glaze

1 Heat the oil in a large, heavy-based pan. Add the onions, season with salt and pepper and cook for about 5–6 minutes until golden. Stir in the garlic, bay leaf and rosemary and cook for a few seconds, then add the lentils, aduki beans and carrots and stir so they are all coated in the juices.

2 Raise the heat and add the ale and stock and let it bubble for a few minutes, then turn the heat down and simmer with the lid on for about 40 minutes, or until the lentils are tender, topping up with hot water as needed. Stir in the mustard and potatoes, taste and season some more if needed.

3 Preheat the oven to 200°C/400°F/Gas 6.

4 To make the pastry, put the flour and a pinch of salt in a large bowl and mix together, then add the sunflower spread and rub in with your fingertips until it resembles breadcrumbs. Trickle in a little ice-cold water, you hardly need any, then pull together and form into a dough.

5 Turn it out onto a lightly floured surface and roll out so it is about 5cm/2in larger than the pie dish. Cut a long strip of pastry to go around the edge of the dish, about 3cm/1¼in deep. Dampen the edges of the pie dish and secure the strip all the way round. This will help to seal the top layer of pastry. Spoon in the lentil mixture. Moisten the pastry strip, then top with the remaining pastry and press to secure and crimp the edges. Make a couple of slits on the top to let steam escape, then brush it with almond milk.

6 Bake for about 30–40 minutes, or until dark golden and the pastry is cooked and crisp. Serve with some steamed savoy cabbage or kale.

Mushroom ragu with home-made pappardelle

This is so rich and 'meaty', no hardened meat-eater would be disappointed. Dried pasta is usually egg-free, but it's nice to make your own every now and again as it is so easy.

Serves 4
Prep: 40 mins Cook: 1½ hours

1 tbsp olive oil
1 onion, finely chopped
2 garlic cloves, finely chopped
a few rosemary stalks, leaves finely
  chopped
200g/7oz chestnut/cremini
  mushrooms, quite finely chopped
2 tbsp dried porcini mushrooms,
  soaked in water for 30 minutes
1 glass of red wine (about 150ml/
  5fl oz/scant ⅔ cup)
500ml/17fl oz/heaped 2 cups
  passata/sieved tomatoes
1 handful of parsley leaves, finely
  chopped, to garnish
sea salt and freshly ground black
  pepper

FOR THE PASTA
400g/14oz/3¼ cups pasta '00' flour,
  sifted
2 tbsp olive oil

1 Heat the oil in a large, heavy-based pan. Add the onion, season with salt and pepper and cook for 2–3 minutes until beginning to soften. Stir in the garlic and cook for a minute more. Add the rosemary and mushrooms, turn to coat and cook for about 3–4 minutes.

2 Drain the porcini, reserving the juice, chop finely and add to the pot. Strain the juice through a fine strainer. Raise the heat, add the wine and bubble for a few minutes. Add the mushroom water, passata/sieved tomatoes and 500ml/ 17fl oz/generous 2 cups of hot water from the kettle. Bring to the boil, then turn the heat down and simmer with the lid partially on for about 1 hour, stirring occasionally and topping up with hot water from the kettle when it needs it. Taste and season some more if needed.

3 While the sauce is cooking, prepare the pasta. Put the flour in a large bowl and add a pinch of salt. Make a well in the middle and very slowly trickle in 200ml/7fl oz/scant 1 cup warm water and the oil, pulling in the flour as you go. Mix until it all comes together as a dough, adding a trickle more water if necessary. Knead for about 10 minutes until it becomes silky and soft. Cover and leave to rest for 10 minutes, then knead it again. Roll out thinly or use a pasta machine and slice into ribbons.

4 To cook, add the pasta to boiling salted water and cook it for about 3–4 minutes, or until it is al dente, then drain well. Toss the pasta with the ragu, then sprinkle with parsley to serve.

For non-vegans...
Finish with a handful of grated Parmesan cheese.

Aloo gobi with tomatoes & cashews

This dish is a real riot of flavour and delicious served with minty yogurt, some mango chutney and your favourite Indian-style vegan bread.

Serves 4
Prep: 15 mins Cook: 50 mins

6 medium-large potatoes, quartered
1 cauliflower, broken into florets
2 red onions, roughly chopped
1 tbsp olive oil
1 tsp coriander seeds, crushed
1 tsp ground turmeric
1 tsp garam masala
1 tsp mustard seeds
5cm/1¾in piece of fresh root ginger,
    peeled and grated
1 red chilli, deseeded and chopped
zest of 1 small orange
6 tomatoes, halved, seeds removed
    and flesh diced
40g/1½oz/⅓ cup cashew nuts,
    toasted
1 handful of coriander/cilantro
    leaves, to garnish
sea salt and freshly ground black
    pepper

FOR THE PICKLED CUCUMBER

2 tbsp rice vinegar
1–2 tsp caster/superfine sugar
½ medium-sized cucumber, seeds
    removed and diced

TO SERVE

250g/9oz/1 cup dairy-free yogurt
1 handful of mint leaves, finely
    chopped, or 1–2 tsp mint sauce
mango chutney
chapattis or roti
lemon wedges

1 Preheat the oven to 200°C/400°F/Gas 6.

2 Put the potatoes, cauliflower and onion in a large roasting pan. It is important there is lots of room so everything roasts rather than steams. Add the olive oil and toss together to coat, then season with salt and pepper and add the spices, ginger, chilli and orange zest. Roast for 30 minutes, then turn the oven down to 180°C/350°F/Gas 6 and cook for a further 10 minutes or so, or until the potatoes are really golden and crisp. Keep an eye on the cauliflower to make sure it doesn't burn.

3 While that's cooking, mix the yogurt with the mint leaves and season to taste with salt and pepper. Set aside.

4 Mix together the rice vinegar and sugar, season with salt and pepper, then toss with the cucumber.

5 Once the potatoes are cooked, remove from the oven, scatter the tomatoes over the dish and stir them in – they will 'cook' a little in the heat. Scatter over the cashew nuts and coriander/cilantro. You can serve from the pan or spoon the potato mixture onto a large serving plate. Serve with the cucumber, mint yogurt, chutney, breads and lemon wedges.

For non-vegans...

Personally I don't think this needs any additions but if you do have some hard-core meat-eating guests to feed, you could cook a leg of lamb in the oven at 160°C/325°F/Gas 3 for 3–4 hours, or until the meat falls off the bone.

Squash, chicory & hazelnut with chermoula

This is an all-in-one roast of many colours and flavours, simple to prep and simple to cook. I love dishes like this as they are so forgiving, you can't really go wrong with them. It is all about the flavour combinations and the Moroccan-style sauce just rounds it all off nicely! I serve this with flatbreads and a leafy salad but for a more substantial meal, serve it with rice or delicious with the Slow-Cooked Lentils with Cider & Rosemary (see page 127).

Serves 6
Prep: 15 mins Cook: 40 mins

2 butternut squash, halved, peeled, deseeded and sliced into half moon shapes
a pinch of allspice
a pinch of chilli flakes
1 tbsp olive oil
2–3 heads of mixed chicory, red and white, bases trimmed and leaves separated
1 large handful of hazelnuts, a few roughly chopped for topping
1 large handful of plump sultanas/ golden raisins
sea salt and freshly ground black pepper

FOR THE CHERMOULA
2 large handfuls of coriander/ cilantro, you can use the stalks and leaves
1 preserved lemon, pith removed, skin finely chopped
a pinch of paprika
2 garlic cloves
1–2 tbsp white wine vinegar
extra virgin olive oil

TO SERVE
flatbreads, to serve
lemon wedges, to serve

1 Preheat the oven to 200°C/400°F/Gas 6.

2 Put the squash in a roasting pan and toss with the allspice, chilli flakes, oil and salt and pepper. Roast for about 20–25 minutes. Add the chicory and cook for 15 minutes more, then add the whole hazelnuts and raisins and cook for a final 5 minutes until the squash is golden and tender. Give the pan a shake, then leave to one side.

3 While that is cooking, put all the chermoula ingredients in a food processor and whiz until well chopped. Season well with salt and pepper and whiz again. Taste and season some more if needed. Leave to one side.

4 Sprinkle the chopped nuts over the squash and dot over the chermoula. Serve with flatbreads and lemon wedges.

For non-vegans...
Scatter the squash with pancetta cubes before putting in the oven.

Courgette, mushroom & truffle oil pizza

Who needs dairy on a pizza? What you need is flavour, and this combo has lots of it. You can make the dough ahead and leave it to prove slowly in the refrigerator for a few days or wrap well and freeze for up to a month. For a change, try tossing a handful of fresh wild rocket/arugula on top to serve and give the pizza an extra drizzle of chilli oil.

Makes 4
Prep: 20 mins, plus proving
Cook: 10 mins

500g/1lb 2oz/4 cups '00' flour or strong white flour, sifted, plus extra for dusting
7g/¼oz/1 sachet of fast-action/instant active dried yeast
4 tbsp olive oil, plus extra for greasing
sea salt

FOR THE TOPPING
8 tbsp passata/sieved tomatoes
300g/10½oz portobello mushrooms, finely sliced
4 courgettes/zucchini, sliced into ribbons
a pinch of chilli flakes
a generous drizzle of truffle oil
1 handful basil leaves, to garnish
a few oregano leaves, to garnish

For non-vegans...

Try any non-vegan topping you like with this base and tomato sauce. It works well with dairy-free cheese, too, but you could scatter over some torn mozarella if you prefer.

1 To make the pizza dough, put the flour, yeast and a pinch of salt in a food mixer. Make a well in the middle and slowly pour in 360ml/12½fl oz/1½ cups of warm water. Using the dough beaters, beat until the mixture comes together, then add 4 tablespoons of olive oil and continue to mix until it forms a dough. It will begin to make a slapping noise as it mixes, which means it is ready. Transfer to a floured board and knead for about 10 minutes until it softens up and becomes spongy.

2 Put the dough in a bowl, cover with cling film/plastic wrap or a dish towel and leave in a warm place for 30–40 minutes until doubled in size.

3 Preheat the oven to its highest setting and put a baking/cookie sheet in the oven to heat up.

4 Turn the dough out onto a lightly floured surface and knead for a couple of minutes to knock out the air, then divide the dough into four equal balls.

5 Have all your topping ingredients ready. Roll and stretch a dough ball until you get a round, about 25cm/10in in diameter. Making one at a time, lightly oil the hot baking/cookie sheet and put the dough round on it. Add 2 tablespoons of passata/sieved tomatoes to the top of the pizza and spread it out to cover. Top with mushrooms and courgettes/zucchini. It will seem like a lot of courgette/zucchini but pile them high as they will shrink when cooking. Sprinkle with chilli flakes and drizzle the truffle oil over the top. Bake for 10 minutes until golden. Remove and continue making the other pizzas. Garnish with fresh herbs, slice into triangles and serve.

Spicy pepper roast with beans & lime yogurt

I love the simplicity of all-in-one dishes, such as this chilli-inspired dish, and the way the flavours meld together in the oven is a kind of delcious alchemy.

Serves 4–6
Prep: 20 mins Cook: 50 mins

6 peppers (a mix of colours works well), deseeded and roughly chopped
2 celery stalks, trimmed and chopped
2 red onions, roughly chopped
4 plump garlic cloves left in skin
1 large handful of cherry tomatoes
a pinch of cayenne pepper
a pinch of ground cinnamon
a pinch of ground cumin
a pinch of dried oregano
1 red chilli, sliced
1 green chilli, sliced
2–3 tbsp olive oil
2 x 400g/14oz cans of kidney beans, drained
4 tbsp passata/sieved tomatoes
a square of dairy-free dark chocolate, 90% cocoa, to grate over the top (optional)
1 handful of coriander/cilantro leaves, to garnish
sea salt and freshly ground black pepper

FOR THE YOGURT
500g/1lb 2oz/4 cups soy yogurt with almond or plain soy yogurt
juice of about 2 limes

TO SERVE
plain cooked brown or white rice
warm pitta breads
lime wedges

1 Preheat the oven to 190°C/375°F/Gas 5.

2 Put the peppers, celery, onions, garlic and tomatoes in a large roasting pan, making sure the vegetables have plenty of room so they roast rather than steam – you may need to use two pans. Add the spices, the oregano and chillies and season well with salt and pepper. Drizzle over the oil and toss really well so everything is coated. Roast for 30–40 minutes until the vegetables are tender and beginning to char.

3 While the vegetables are cooking, put the kidney beans in a pan with the passata/sieved tomatoes and simmer gently for about 10–15 minutes, then spoon them over the roasting vegetables and turn to coat for the last 10 minutes of cooking.

4 Meanwhile, mix the yogurt with the lime juice and add a pinch of salt to taste – you are looking for it to be fairly sharpish and sour.

5 To serve, spoon out the roasted mix into shallow bowls, grate over the chocolate, if using, and sprinkle with the coriander/cilantro leaves. Serve with the yogurt, rice, warm pitta breads and lime wedges alongside.

For non-vegans...
Take the chilli flavours one step further by stirring in some sliced or shredded cooked beef in with the roasted vegetables for the last 10 minutes of cooking.

New potatoes, freekeh, pecan & preserved lemons with mustard & saffron dressing

I am a big fan of freekeh and often choose it to cook with. It is wheat, albeit a young green one, so if you wish to go gluten-free, choose quinoa instead for this recipe, although quinoa doesn't have quite the same nuttiness.

Serves 6
Prep: 15 mins Cook: 40 mins

900g/2lb new potatoes, halved
2 tbsp olive oil
1 red onion, finely chopped
2 garlic cloves, finely chopped
a pinch of sumac
400g/14oz/2 cups freekeh
700ml/24fl oz/2¾ cups hot
  vegetable stock
1 large handful of pecan nuts,
  roughly chopped
4 preserved lemons, halved, pith
  removed, flesh roughly chopped
1 handful of dill fronds, chopped
1 handful of flatleaf parsley leaves,
  chopped
1 large handful of pomegranate
  seeds
sea salt and freshly ground black
  pepper

FOR THE DRESSING
300g/10½oz/1¼ cups soy yogurt
2–3 tsp Dijon mustard
a few strands of saffron, soaked in a
  little warm water for 5 minutes
1 tsp maple syrup

1 Preheat the oven to 200°C/400°F/Gas 6.

2 Put the potatoes in a roasting pan, add half the oil and season with salt and pepper, then toss together using your hands. Roast for about 30–40 minutes, or until the potatoes are golden and tender.

3 While the potatoes are cooking, heat the remaining oil in a large, heavy-based pan. Add the onion, season with salt and pepper and cook for 2–3 minutes until softened. Stir in the garlic and sumac and cook for a few seconds, then stir in the freekeh until it absorbs all the juices. Pour in the stock, bring to the boil, then turn the heat down and simmer for about 12 minutes, stirring occasionally, until all the stock has been absorbed and the freekeh is tender, topping up with hot water from the kettle if needed.

4 To make the dressing, mix the yogurt with the mustard, saffron and the maple syrup and season well to taste with salt and pepper. You can add a little of the water from the saffron to thin down the dressing, if necessary. Leave to one side.

5 Add the pecan nuts and preserved lemons to the potatoes in the roasting pan for the last 10–15 minutes of cooking. Remove from the oven, tip in the freekeh and stir so everything is coated, then scatter over the herbs and stir again. Now sprinkle the pomegranate seeds over the top.

6 To serve, spoon the freekeh mixture into shallow bowls, then dollop over a little dressing to serve.

Sweet potato goulash with caraway

This is more like a stew than the Hungarian-style goulash, which is more soupy. Adding vinegar to the pot gives it a fabulous sourness, and roasting the sweet potatoes first in the paprika adds huge depth of flavour to the dish.

Serves 4
Prep: 20 mins Cook: 1 hour

500g/1lb 2oz sweet potatoes,
    peeled and cubed
2 tbsp olive oil
1 tbsp plain/all-purpose flour
1 tbsp smoked paprika, plus extra
    for topping
1 onion, finely chopped
2 garlic cloves, finely chopped
2 tsp caraway seeds
2 celery stalks, diced
2 carrots, peeled and diced
1 red pepper, deseeded and finely
    diced
1 green pepper, deseeded and
    roughly chopped
2 tbsp white wine vinegar
400g/14oz can of chopped tomatoes
1 handful of flatleaf parsley leaves,
    finely chopped, to garnish
sea salt and freshly ground black
    pepper

FOR THE SOUR CREAM
about 350g/12oz pack of silken tofu
juice of 1 lemon
a splash of rice vinegar

1 Preheat the oven to 200°C/400°F/Gas 6.

2 Toss the sweet potatoes with half of the oil, season with salt and pepper, then toss with the flour and paprika. Put in a roasting pan and roast for about 20 minutes, or until tender.

3 Heat the remaining oil in a large, heavy-based pan. Add the onion, season with salt and pepper and cook for 2–3 minutes until beginning to soften. Stir in the garlic, caraway seeds, celery, carrots and red pepper and cook on low heat for about 10–15 minutes, then stir in the green pepper and cook for 5 minutes more. Raise the heat, add the vinegar and bubble until evaporated, then tip in the tomatoes and three cans of hot water. Bring to the boil, then reduce to a bubbling simmer and cook for about 15 minutes. Stir in the sweet potatoes, taste and season some more if needed.

4 While that is cooking, put the silken tofu, lemon juice, rice vinegar and a pinch of salt in a blender and blitz until combined. Taste and add more salt or lemon juice if needed.

5 To serve, ladle the goulash into shallow bowls, scatter the parsley over the top and serve with rice, a spoonful of the 'sour cream' and a sprinkle of paprika.

For non-vegans...
Beef is the obvious ingredient to add if you are feeding meat-eaters. Fry up 450g/1lb of beef skirt, roughly chopped, and add it to the carrot and celery mix. It may need a longer cooking time until the beef is fork tender.

Fig, broccoli & sweet potato with pomegranate & harissa yogurt

This is a magnificent traybake roast that can be served with brown rice for a complete meal. Purple sprouting broccoli looks the part but if it is not in season use regular broccoli. If you've not roasted olives before, enjoy, as they take on a whole new flavour.

Serves 4–6
Prep: 10 mins Cook: 40 mins

300g/10½oz/2 cups basmati brown rice
6 large sweet potatoes, roughly chopped or cut into wedges
a drizzle of pomegranate molasses
2 tbsp olive oil
400g/14oz purple sprouting broccoli, chunky stalks trimmed
8 figs
4 limes, roughly chopped
1 handful of green olives
1 green chilli, finely sliced
1 handful of flaked/slivered almonds, toasted
1 handful of pumpkin seeds, toasted
1 handful of coriander/cilantro leaves, chopped
1 handful of pomegranate seeds
2 tsp nigella seeds
sea salt and freshly ground black pepper

FOR THE HARISSA YOGURT
300g/10½oz/scant 1¼ cups soy yogurt with almond or plain soy
1 tbsp harissa, to taste

1 Preheat the oven to 200°C/400°F/Gas 6.

2 Put the rice in a pan, add twice as much water and a pinch of salt and bring to the boil. Turn the heat down and simmer with the lid on for about 25–30 minutes, or until tender and the water has been absorbed. Fluff up with a fork.

3 Toss the sweet potatoes with the pomegranate molasses and half the oil, season with salt and pepper and put in a large roasting pan. Toss the broccoli, figs and limes in the remaining oil and add them to the pan, then roast for about 10–15 minutes. Add the olives, green chilli, almonds and pumpkin seeds and cook for 10–15 minutes more, or until the potatoes are golden.

4 While the dish is in the oven, mix together the yogurt and harissa and season with salt. Sprinkle the roast vegetables with the coriander/cilantro, pomegranate and nigella seeds and serve with the rice and yogurt on the side.

For non-vegans...
Crumble some good-quality feta over the roast vegetables along with the herbs, pomegranate and nigella seeds – it works particularly well with the roasted olives.

Vegan pad Thai

This is really quick and easy to make but do make sure you use the right noodles as it makes all the difference to the finished dish. When you are cooking a stir-fry, make it easy for yourself and get all the ingredients out, measured and ready, so you can add them straight to the wok.

Serves 4
Prep: 15 mins Cook: 25 mins

400g/14oz/3⅓ cups firm tofu, cut
    into cubes
200g/7oz flat rice stick noodles
1–3 tbsp groundnut oil
a bunch of spring onions/scallions,
    trimmed and finely chopped
2 garlic cloves, finely chopped
2 carrots, peeled into ribbons
a pinch of chilli flakes
120g/4¼oz/scant 1 cup roasted
    peanuts, finely chopped
300g/10½oz/3 cups bean sprouts
1 handful of fresh coriander/cilantro
    leaves, finely chopped
lime wedges, to serve
sea salt and freshly ground black
    pepper

FOR THE SAUCE
2 tbsp palm sugar or demerara/
    turbinado sugar
2 tbsp rice vinegar
6 tsp tamarind paste
juice of 1 lime

For non-vegans...
Add some large uncooked
prawns/shrimp to the wok at
the end of cooking and cook
for 4–5 minutes, until pink.

1 Crumble a quarter of the tofu cubes and put them to one side. Soak the noodles in boiling water for 10 minutes.

2 To make the sauce, mix all the ingredients together until the sugar has dissolved, and season to taste with salt and pepper. Leave to one side.

3 Heat the oil in a wok, add the cubed tofu and stir-fry until golden and crisp (you may need to do this in batches), adding more oil as required. This may take 10–15 minutes. Remove with a slotted spoon and leave to one side.

4 Add a little more oil to the pan, if needed. Add the spring onions/scallions, season with salt and pepper and stir around the pan for a minute or so, then add the garlic and cook for a few seconds more, being careful that it doesn't burn. Add the carrots and chilli flakes and cook for a minute or so, then add the reserved crumbled tofu and stir it around the pan until it looks like it has scrambled.

5 Drain the noodles and add to the pan. Push everything to one side and add the sauce, let it bubble, then incorporate it into the pan so the noodles are coated. Add half the peanuts, half the coriander/cilantro and half the bean sprouts and turn to coat, then return the cooked tofu to the pan and stir well. Taste and add more lime juice or chilli flakes if needed.

6 Transfer to serving dishes and top with the remaining bean sprouts, peanuts and coriander/cilantro to serve, with some lime wedges on the side.

5

SIDES

Paprika roast potatoes with fennel & olives

Knowing how to make good roast potatoes is an important part of your cooking repertoire. This is a basic recipe for roasties with a few added ingredients thrown in later on in the cooking so as to use just the one roasting pan. For potatoes that are crisp on the outside and fluffy in the middle, you need hot oil and for the potatoes to be nice and dry – the flour coating helps to make the outside gorgeous and crisp.

Serves 4–6
Prep: 15 mins
Cook: 1 hour 20 mins

1kg/2lb 4oz potatoes, such as
    Maris Piper, peeled and cut into
    even-sized pieces
sea salt
about 4–5 tbsp olive oil or
    rapeseed oil
1 tbsp plain/all-purpose flour
1 tbsp paprika
1 large fennel bulb, trimmed and
    roughly chopped
1 large handful of black olives

1 Put the potatoes in a pan of salted water and bring to the boil, then turn down the heat and simmer for about 6–8 minutes – you don't want them to get too soft. Drain well and return to the pan, put the lid on and leave them to dry out for a few minutes.

2 While the potatoes are cooking, preheat the oven to 200°C/400°F/Gas 6. Put 4 tablespoons of oil in a large roasting pan, put it in the oven and leave it to get really hot.

3 Mix together the flour and paprika, sprinkle the mixture over the potatoes and, with the lid on, give the pan a good shake so they all get lightly coated. Now add the potatoes to the hot oil, being careful that it doesn't splash. Sprinkle with salt and roast for about 25–30 minutes.

4 Toss the fennel and olives with the remaining oil and add to the roasting pan, tucking it all in between the potatoes. Return to the oven for a further 40–50 minutes, or until the potatoes are crisp and golden.

For non-vegans...

If you prefer, you can roast the potatoes in a large knob of goose fat, rather than the olive oil.

Slow-cooked lentils with cider & rosemary

We eat a lot of lentils at my house. I fell in love with them in Italy as we travel to the Abruzzo quite frequently and the lentils from there are amazing. Dare I say better than Puy lentils? Anyway, we bring lots of packs home, and if you can get them from an Italian deli they really are worth a try. This dish is good served alongside the Vegan Sausages (see page 28) or with any of the one-pan roasts. To turn this into a soup, simply increase the stock. It also tastes fabulous with some chopped vacuum-packed chestnuts stirred into it.

Serves 4–6
Prep: 10 mins Cook: 1 hour

1 tbsp olive oil
1 onion, finely chopped
1 carrot, finely diced
1 celery stalk, finely diced
2 garlic cloves, finely chopped
a few rosemary stalks, leaves finely
    chopped
400g/14oz/2 cups Puy lentils or
    lentils from the Abruzzo
300ml/10½fl oz/1¼ cups dry cider
about 900ml/31fl oz/3¾ cups hot
    vegetable stock
sea salt and freshly ground black
    pepper

1 Heat the oil over a medium heat in a large, heavy-based pan, add the onion, season with salt and pepper and cook for 2–3 minutes until softened. Stir in the carrot and celery and cook for about 6–8 minutes, stirring occasionally so they don't catch and burn. Stir in the garlic, rosemary and lentils, and cook for a few seconds more then raise the heat, add the cider and let it bubble for a couple of minutes.

2 Pour in most of the stock, let it bubble, then turn the heat down and simmer with the lid partially on for about 35–40 minutes, or until the lentils are tender. Top up with more stock as it cooks for your preferred consistency. Taste and season some more if needed.

For non-vegans...

Add some pancetta cubes with the carrot and celery to cook. These lentils make a delicious accompaniment to cooked, sliced belly pork.

Potato salad with peas, capers & gherkins

This is much healthier than a potato salad made with mayonnaise. Peas add sweetness and capers and gherkins add some real tang. I prefer using new potatoes in their skin, for the taste and the ease. Leave the potatoes whole to cook as they will cook evenly and retain their flavour, then leave to cool completely before cutting them into chunks.

Serves 4–6
Prep: 15 mins Cook: 20 mins

700g/1lb 9oz new potatoes
100g/4oz/¾ cup frozen peas
1 fennel bulb, trimmed and finely shredded, fronds reserved
1 bunch of spring onions/scallions, trimmed and finely chopped
3 tsp capers
1 large gherkin or a few cornichons, finely sliced
200g/7oz/scant 1 cup soy yogurt
sea salt and freshly ground black pepper
1 handful of flatleaf parsley, leaves finely chopped

1 Put the potatoes in a pan of salted water and bring to the boil, then turn the heat down and simmer for about 15 minutes, or until fork tender. Drain and leave to cool, then cut into bite-sized pieces.

2 Bring a second pan of salted water to the boil, add the peas and cook for 2–3 minutes, then drain and refresh in cold water.

3 Put the potatoes, fennel, spring onions/scallions, capers and gherkins in a large bowl and tip in the peas. Spoon in the yogurt and stir gently so everything is coated. Season with salt and pepper, add the parsley and turn to coat. Garnish with fennel fronds to serve.

Chilli & orange carrots with herby breadcrumbs

Eating roasted carrots is like eating a completely different vegetable from boiled ones.
You need to make plenty as they tend to shrink on cooking. If you use the little Chantenay
carrots, you won't need to peel them. I always have breadcrumbs in the freezer so I can
use them straight from frozen when I want to cook a recipe like this. It may sound a little
worthy but once you get into the habit of blitzing any leftover bread and popping it in the
freezer, you'll wonder how you managed before!

Serves 4
Prep: 20 mins Cook: 25 mins

500g/1lb Chantenay carrots,
    trimmed
1 tbsp olive oil
seeds from 4 cardamom pods,
    crushed
1 green chilli, deseeded and finely
    chopped
zest of 1 orange and juice of ½
1 handful of fresh breadcrumbs
1 handful of flatleaf parsley leaves,
    finely chopped
sea salt and freshly ground black
    pepper
a few thyme leaves, to garnish

1 Preheat the oven to 200°C/400°F/Gas 6.

2 Put the carrots in a large roasting pan, drizzle in the olive
oil, add the cardamom seeds, chilli, half the orange zest and
the orange juice and season with salt and pepper. Using your
hands, toss it all together so it is all coated. Roast for about
20 minutes, or until tender and golden.

3 While the carrots are cooking, put the breadcrumbs, the
remaining orange zest and the parsley in a frying pan and
cook for a few minutes until golden and crisp. Transfer the
carrots to a serving dish, sprinkle over the breadcrumbs and
top with the thyme leaves to serve.

Artichokes, peas & broad beans

This is a big cheat as it uses artichokes from a jar, but it works and is super-tasty for a side dish to some roasties or a lightly dressed salad. Cook everything until it is a little charred to add lots of flavour, then add a drizzle of red wine vinegar to give it some acidity. Don't waste the oil from the artichokes – save it to use in a dressing. For a change, you could scatter some toasted breadcrumbs over the top.

Serves 4
Prep: 5 mins Cook: 20 mins

300g/10½oz/2½ cups frozen broad/
    fava beans
1 tbsp olive oil
1 onion, finely chopped
2 garlic cloves, finely chopped
285g/10oz jar of artichokes,
    drained, any large ones halved
200g/7oz/1½ cups frozen peas,
    defrosted
1 tbsp red wine vinegar
1 handful of flatleaf parsley leaves,
    finely chopped
sea salt and freshly ground black
    pepper

1 Put the broad/fava beans in a bowl of hot water for 5–6 minutes, then drain and skin.

2 While they are soaking, heat the oil in a large frying pan, add the onion, season well with salt and pepper and cook for 2–3 minutes until softened. Add the garlic and cook for a few seconds more. Stir in the artichokes, peas and broad/fava beans and cook on a fairly high heat for about 10 minutes, stirring occasionally, until the mixture begins to char slightly.

3 With the heat high, add the vinegar and continue cooking until the vinegar smell has disappeared. Taste and season if needed, then spoon into a serving dish and scatter over the parsley to serve.

For non-vegans...

While the artichokes, peas and beans are cooking, slice 4 rashers of bacon into thin strips. Melt a knob of butter in a frying pan, add the bacon pieces and fry for 2–3 minutes until crispy. Scatter over the vegetables with the parsley.

Roasted onions with squash & pine nut stuffing

Onions make the perfect case for a rich and robust stuffing mix. This is great as a side dish with roast potatoes and veggies or it could take centre stage with a lightly dressed salad and some crusty bread on the side. I always pre-cook my onions before roasting them as it results in a fabulous silky texture.

Serves 4
Prep: 20 mins Cook: 40 mins

8 large red onions
1 small butternut squash, halved, peeled, deseeded and cubed
2 tbsp olive oil
2 garlic cloves, finely chopped
1 tsp Dijon mustard
2 tsp ground cinnamon
100g/3½oz/1⅔ cups fresh breadcrumbs
1 handful of flatleaf parsley leaves, finely chopped, plus extra to garnish
1 handful of pine nuts
sea salt and freshly ground black pepper

1 Preheat the oven to 200°C/400°F/Gas 6. Trim the tops off the onions, leaving the roots fairly intact to hold the onion together.

2 Put the squash in a roasting pan, drizzle over 1 tablespoon of the oil and season with salt and pepper. Roast for about 20 minutes, or until fork tender, then leave to cool a little and chop into smaller pieces.

3 Bring a large pan of water to the boil, add the onions and cook for about 10 minutes, or until almost tender. Remove the onions with a slotted spoon and, when cool enough to handle, remove the onion middle with your fingers – it should slip out when pushed. Finely chop this and leave to one side. Place the onions in a lightly oiled roasting pan.

4 Heat the remaining oil in a large frying pan, add the reserved chopped onion, the garlic and squash and cook for a few minutes, stirring to combine. Stir in the mustard, cinnamon, breadcrumbs and parsley and season well with salt and pepper. If it is at all dry, add a little hot water from the kettle until it binds together.

5 Now scoop up the mixture and use it to fill the onions, packing them as much as you can (there may be some left over but you can always roll it into balls and fry). Cover the onions with kitchen foil and bake for about 15 minutes, then remove the foil and bake for 15 minutes more. Scatter over the pine nuts and cook until golden. Scatter the remaining parsley over the top to serve.

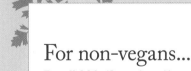

For non-vegans...

Fry off 200g/8oz minced/ground pork with the filling ingredients, making sure it is cooked through before filling the onions.

Asparagus with shallots in raspberry vinegar

I love the taste of griddled asparagus. This has got to be my favourite way of cooking it, and it's a whole lot easier to get right than by boiling it. The dressing marries so well with the sweet and charred flavours of the asparagus – it makes a super-easy side dish, especially in the spring. Choose medium-sized asparagus for this; thin ones will overcook and char too quickly and the thick ones aren't as sophisticated for this dish.

Serves 4
Prep: 10 mins Cook: 10 mins

550g/1lb 4oz medium asparagus, trimmed
1–2 tbsp olive oil
sea salt and freshly ground black pepper
a few mint leaves, to garnish

FOR THE DRESSING
6 shallots, very finely sliced
4 tbsp raspberry vinegar
a pinch of caster/superfine sugar

1 First make the dressing. Put the shallots in a bowl. Mix together the raspberry vinegar and sugar until the sugar has dissolved, then season well with salt and pepper. Pour it over the shallots and stir well. Leave to one side.

2 Heat a griddle pan to hot. Toss the asparagus in the oil and season with salt and pepper. Add the asparagus to the pan, but don't over-fill – you will need to cook it in batches. Cook for a couple of minutes, or until char lines appear, then turn and cook the other side for about the same time, or until the asparagus is tender. Transfer to a serving dish and continue cooking all the asparagus.

3 To serve, drizzle as much of the dressing as you want over the asparagus – you may not need or want all of it – and scatter over the mint leaves.

Steamed greens & kimchi

This dish is a great example of how, with a little bit of extra love, something really simple can be elevated to something truly special. The addition of kimchi brings salt and spice to a modest serving of steamed green vegetables, transforming it into a moreish and memorable side dish in the process.

Serves 4
Prep: 5 mins Cook: 15 mins

1 head of broccoli, cut into florets, or about 400g/14oz Tenderstem broccoli, trimmed
1 handful of chard, stalks chopped and leaves roughly chopped
4 tbsp Kimchi (see page 173), chopped
2 lemons, cut into wedges, to serve
sea salt

1 Steam the broccoli and chard stalks with a pinch of salt in a steamer or put them in a metal colander set over a pan of simmering water. Cover and cook for about 10 minutes, then add the chard leaves and cook for 5 minutes more.

2 Transfer to a serving dish and serve with lemon wedges for squeezing and a little chopped kimchi alongside.

For non-vegans...
This would make a good dish to serve with griddled lamb.

Mixed greens with red pepper sauce

A red pepper sauce works with so many different veggies or tossed with pasta – I like the taste of earthy greens with a sweet rich sauce. This type of sauce is often served with stuffed cabbage but this is much simpler.

Serves 4
Prep: 5 mins Cook: 40 mins

1 Savoy or dark green cabbage, halved, trimmed and roughly shredded
200g/7oz fine green beans, trimmed
200g/7oz /1½ cups frozen peas, defrosted

FOR THE RED PEPPER SAUCE
3 red peppers
2 tbsp olive oil
3 shallots, finely chopped
2 garlic cloves, finely chopped
about 300ml/10½fl oz/1¼ cups hot vegetable stock
a trickle of red wine vinegar
sea salt and freshly ground black pepper

1 Preheat the oven to 200°C/400°F/Gas 6.

2 First make the red pepper sauce. Put the peppers in a roasting pan, smother with a little of the oil and roast for about 30–40 minutes, or until charred. When cool enough to handle, remove the skin from the peppers. Halve and deseed them, then leave to one side.

3 While the peppers are cooking, heat the remaining oil in a large frying pan, add the shallots, season with salt and pepper and cook for 2–3 minutes until softened. Stir in the garlic and cook for a few seconds more.

4 Put the peeled peppers, shallot and garlic mix and a few ladles of the stock into a blender and whiz until you have a thick, smooth sauce, adding a little more stock if needed. Pour it back into the frying pan with the vinegar and reheat. Taste and season as it needs it.

5 Meanwhile, steam the cabbage in a steamer or sit it in a metal colander, add a pinch of salt, and cook with the lid on over a pan of simmering water for about 5–10 minutes. Add the beans and peas and cook for 10 minutes more, or until the cabbage is tender.

6 Drain the greens really well and transfer to a serving dish. Spoon over the pepper sauce or serve it on the side.

For non-vegans...

These greens are a delicious accompaniment to roasted haddock or other firm white fish. Drizzle 500g/1lb 2oz haddock fillet with olive oil, season and roast in the oven for about 15 minutes, until opaque and cooked through.

Wasabi sweet potato chips

These are hot but moreish – make them to eat as a snack on their own or serve as a side dish.
Go easy on the wasabi – you can always add a little more but it packs a real punch, and
the chips/fries should have just a subtle heat, not blow your head off! Don't cut the sweet
potatoes too thinly or they may burn and become too crisp in the oven. Make sure they have
lots of room in a large roasting pan, as if they are crowded they will steam rather than roast.

Serves 4
Prep: 15 mins Cook: 25 mins

1 kg/2lb 4oz sweet potato, peeled
    and sliced into thick fingers
¼–½ tsp wasabi paste
1–2 tbsp olive oil
sea salt
a few parsley leaves, roughly
    chopped, to garnish

1 Preheat the oven to 200°C/400°F/Gas 6.

2 Put the sweet potatoes in a large roasting pan. Mix the
wasabi with the oil, whisking with a fork. Drizzle it over the
chips/fries and toss together using your hands, then sprinkle
evenly with salt and roast for 20–25 minutes, or until crisp
and golden.

3 Sprinkle with parsley to serve.

6

SALADS

Farro, spinach, shallots & broad beans

Roasted baby onions turn this into a really substantial main-meal salad – their sweetness is so good with the grains. If you weep at the thought of peeling baby onions, don't. Top and tail each one then grab your sunglasses to peel – there will be no tears!

Serves 4–6
Prep: 15 mins Cook: 40 mins

250g/9oz/1½ cups of farro or your favourite grain
1 large handful of mint leaves, chopped, plus extra whole leaves to garnish
a pinch of chilli flakes
400g/14oz shallots (about 26 shallots), peeled
1 tbsp olive oil
a few thyme stalks, leaves picked, plus extra to garnish
300g/10½oz/2½ cups fresh or frozen broad/fava beans, defrosted
1 handful of fresh or frozen peas, defrosted
200g/7oz bag of baby spinach leaves
sea salt and freshly ground black pepper
lemon slices, to garnish

FOR THE DRESSING
3 tbsp extra virgin olive oil
1 tbsp white wine vinegar
1 tsp Dijon mustard
a pinch of sugar (optional)

For non-vegans...
The tanginess of crumbled feta would be great sprinkled over this salad.

1 Preheat the oven to 200°C/400°F/Gas 6.

2 Put the farro in a saucepan, cover with cold water, add a pinch of salt and bring to the boil, then turn the heat down and simmer with the lid on for 20–30 minutes until tender. Drain and, while still warm, mix with the mint and chilli flakes and season well with salt and pepper.

3 While the grain is cooking, put the shallots in a large roasting pan, toss with olive oil and thyme leaves and season well with salt and pepper. Roast for about 20 minutes, or until the shallots just start to split and turn golden. Tip the grains into the pan and stir to coat. Leave to one side.

4 Bring a pan of salted water to the boil, add the broad/fava beans and peas, and cook for about 3–4 minutes until tender. Drain well, then peel away the skin from the broad/fava beans, if using frozen (this is totally optional – but I think they are nicer peeled and a great colour). Add the beans and peas to the grains and onions and stir, then stir in the spinach leaves. They will begin to wilt slightly in the heat of the roasting pan.

5 To make the dressing, whisk together the oil, vinegar and mustard, taste and add a pinch of sugar if needed. Season well to taste with salt and pepper.

6 Transfer the salad mixture to a large shallow serving bowl, drizzle over the dressing, leaving a little on the table for extra serving. Garnish with lemon slices and the remaining mint leaves and thyme.

Nearly niçoise

You need really juicy tomatoes and good black olives for this. The capers and gherkins add the piquancy and punch that this salad needs without the traditional anchovies. It's fresh and flavoursome and makes an interesting lunch with some good bread.

Serves 4
Prep: 10 mins Cook: 15 mins

500g/1lb 2oz new potatoes
320g/11¼oz pack of fine green
    beans, trimmed
2 baby gem lettuce, leaves
    separated, washed and dried
3 tsp baby capers
4–6 tomatoes, roughly chopped
280g/10oz jar of artichokes in
    oil, drained and any large ones
    halved
1 handful of pitted black olives
1 handful of fresh flatleaf parsley
    leaves, finely chopped
sea salt and freshly ground black
    pepper

FOR THE DRESSING
3 tbsp extra virgin olive oil
1 tbsp red wine vinegar
2 garlic cloves, grated
1 tsp baby gherkins, crushed
1 tsp Dijon mustard

1 Put the potatoes in a pan of salted water and bring to the boil, then turn the heat down and simmer for 15 minutes, or until fork tender. Drain well and leave to one side to cool. Cut the potatoes into halves, if you like.

2 Bring a pan of salted water to the boil, add the green beans, then simmer for 4–5 minutes until just tender – they still need a bite to them. Drain well and rinse under cold water. This will stop them cooking any further and help to retain their colour. Put to one side in a bowl of cold water and drain before using.

3 To make the dressing, whisk all the ingredients together, then season to taste with salt and pepper.

4 To assemble, put the lettuce in a large bowl with the cooled potatoes and beans. Now add the capers, tomatoes, artichokes and olives and, using your hands, gently tumble it all together.

5 Don't dress the salad until you are ready to serve or the leaves will wilt in an instant. Transfer it to a shallow serving dish, then sprinkle over the parsley and drizzle with the dressing.

For non-vegans...
For a more traditional niçoise, add 6–8 anchovies to the salad and 4 hard-boiled eggs, or perhaps some flaked tuna.

Artichoke, pea, radish, potato & beetroot salad with ginger & sherry dressing

This is a big, blousy salad with lots of colour and texture. The baby roasted potatoes elevate it into a main meal.

Serves 4
Prep: 15 mins   Cook: 30 mins

900g/2lb baby new potatoes, halved
1 tbsp olive oil
1 large handful of fresh or frozen
    peas, defrosted
200g/7oz baby spinach leaves
2 large raw beetroots/beets, grated
200g/7oz radishes, sliced
285g/10oz jar of artichokes,
    drained, reserving the oil
sea salt and freshly ground black
    pepper

FOR THE DRESSING
3 tbsp extra virgin olive oil (or
    use the reserved oil from the
    artichokes)
1 tbsp sherry vinegar
1 handful of chives, finely chopped

1 Preheat the oven to 200°C/400°F/Gas 6.

2 Put the potatoes in a roasting pan, add the oil and season well with salt and pepper. Toss to coat, then roast for about 20–30 minutes, or until golden and tender. Remove and leave to one side.

3 While the potatoes are cooking, mix together the ingredients for the dressing, season with salt and pepper and leave to one side.

4 Cook the peas in a pan of boiling salted water for about 3–4 minutes until tender, then drain and refresh in cold water.

5 To assemble the salad, put the potatoes, spinach leaves and beetroot/beet in a large bowl, add most of the dressing and toss together to coat. Transfer to a serving bowl or dish, scatter over the peas, radishes and artichokes, drizzle with the remaining dressing and serve.

For non-vegans...
Cook 2 chicken breasts in a light stock for about 15–20 minutes, or until cooked through. Remove, and when cool enough to handle, shred the chicken and add to the salad.

Griddled aubergine with caramelized pecan nuts and mint & orange dressing

Aubergine/eggplant is another vegetable like courgette/zucchini that just tastes better griddled or put on the barbecue. This recipe is a good one to double up on and cook for friends as it will sit patiently, the flavours just getting better. The sweet dressing complements the smoky flavours so well – transporting you to summer holidays, whatever the season. Don't slice the aubergine/eggplant too thick or too thin, about 2cm/¾in is the perfect thickness.

Serves 4
Prep: 10 mins Cook: 20 mins

1 handful of pecan nuts
2–3 tsp maple syrup
4 aubergine/eggplants, sliced
    lengthways
about 1 tbsp olive oil

FOR THE DRESSING
6 tbsp extra virgin olive oil (a nice
    fruity one)
juice of 1 orange
2 tbsp white wine vinegar
1 handful of mint leaves, finely
    chopped, plus some whole leaves
    to garnish
a pinch of sugar
1 tsp Dijon mustard (optional but I
    like the tang)
sea salt and freshly ground black
    pepper

1 First cook the nuts. Toss them with the maple syrup, then put them in a small non-stick frying pan and heat through, turning to coat for a minute or so until they begin to caramelize. Remove from the heat and, when cool enough to handle, chop the nuts and leave to one side.

2 Now make the dressing so it can sit to allow the flavours to develop. Put the oil, orange juice and vinegar in a bowl or jug and whisk well, adding salt and pepper to taste. Add the mint, sugar and mustard, if using, and whisk again. Let it stand, then taste and season some more just before serving if needed.

3 Heat a griddle pan to hot, brush the aubergine/eggplant slices with oil, lightly season them, then add a few to the pan at a time, cook for a few minutes, or until char lines appear underneath but try not to move them at first. They are best left to cook undisturbed. Turn and cook the other sides until lightly charred. Continue until you have cooked all the slices.

4 Lay them out on a large serving platter, drizzle over the dressing and scatter over the nuts. Garnish with whole mint leaves to serve.

Roasted cauliflower & broccoli salad with tahini

This is so much more than a salad. It's a meal on its own or a great side dish. Cauliflower has become a popular vegetable since we all started roasting and chargrilling it, the flavour transforms into something intensely sweet and nutty – and broccoli roasted isn't half bad either. The tahini dressing needs a little sweetness, hence the addition of orange juice.

Serves 4
Prep: 15 mins Cook: 30 mins

1 large cauliflower, broken into
     florets, and a few chunky leaves
1 large head of broccoli, broken into
     florets, and a few chunky stalks,
     roughly chopped
2 tbsp olive oil
1 handful of flaked/slivered
     almonds, toasted
2 tsp black sesame seeds
orange wedges, to garnish
sea salt and freshly ground black
     pepper

FOR THE DRESSING
3 tbsp tahini
juice of ½–1 orange
1 garlic clove, grated

1 Preheat the oven to 200°C/400°F/Gas 6.

2 Put the cauliflower and broccoli in a large roasting pan, drizzle over the oil and season with salt and pepper, tossing to coat. Roast for about 20–30 minutes, or until beginning to char. Remove and leave to one side.

3 While the vegetables are roasting, make the dressing. Put the tahini, orange juice and garlic in a bowl and mix well, then add 3–4 tablespoons of water and whisk until smooth, adding a little more water as needed until you get the right consistency. Taste and season well with salt and pepper.

4 Transfer the cauliflower and broccoli to a shallow serving bowl, drizzle over the dressing and toss lightly, then sprinkle over the almonds and black sesame seeds and serve garnished with orange wedges.

Roasted squash & chilli with sumac tomatoes

This is a huge jumble of fantastic flavours. Dairy-free cheese works really well grated and baked with the croûtons. If fresh horseradish is available, I like to grate a little over the squash before roasting, along with the green chilli for added heat. Do add the vinegar mix while the squash is still warm as the flavours will penetrate better.

Serves 4
Prep: 15 mins Cook: 40 mins

1 large butternut squash, halved, peeled, deseeded and sliced into wedges
2 tbsp olive oil
1–2 green chillies, deseeded and finely chopped (depending on your heat preference)
200g/7oz sourdough bread, cut into chunky pieces
a pinch of dried oregano
300g/10½oz cherry tomatoes
a pinch of sumac
1 handful of flatleaf parsley leaves, finely chopped
sea salt and freshly ground black pepper
a few basil leaves, to garnish
a pinch of chilli flakes (optional)
wild rocket/arugula leaf salad, to serve (optional)

FOR THE DRESSING
1 tbsp red wine vinegar
1 tsp demerara/turbinado sugar

1 Preheat the oven to 200°C/400°F/Gas 6.

2 First make the dressing. Whisk together the vinegar and sugar and season to taste with salt and pepper. Leave to one side.

3 Put the squash in a large roasting pan, drizzle with half the oil, season with salt and pepper and scatter the chilli over the top. Using your hands, toss everything together until coated, then roast for 20 minutes.

4 While that's roasting, toss the sourdough with the remaining oil and oregano. Add this to the roasting pan and cook for 10–15 minutes more. Toss the tomatoes with the sumac, add to the pan and cook for 5 minutes more.

5 Sprinkle with the parsley and drizzle with the dressing, leave for a few minutes for the flavours to mingle, then tumble everything together. Sprinkle over the basil leaves and chilli flakes, if using. Transfer to a serving plate or large shallow bowl or serve straight from the roasting pan. Serve with a lightly dressed wild rocket/arugula leaf salad.

For non-vegans...

For any meat-eating guests, serve with good-quality roasted sausages – cooked at 200°C/400°F/Gas 6 for 30 minutes, or until golden and cooked though.

Indonesian rice salad with nuts & papaya

This fried rice salad is kept nice and fresh with the addition of fruit. Tofu is optional but it's good to add if you are serving this as a main-meal salad. If you have any leftover rice in the refrigerator, this makes life even easier, not just because you don't have to cook it, but also the grains will be cold and separated, which is perfect for this type of dish.

Serves 4–6
Prep: 10 mins Cook: 45 mins

450g/1lb/2½ cups basmati rice, washed, or use leftover cold rice
about 3–4 tbsp vegetable oil
300g/10½oz/2½ cups firm tofu, cubed
about 3 tsp kecap manis sauce
1 bunch of spring onions/scallions, green and white parts, trimmed and chopped
2 garlic cloves, finely chopped
1 tsp sambal oelak (use more if you like it really hot), or use a finely chopped red chilli
sea salt
1 large handful of macadamia nuts, toasted and chopped
2 papaya, halved, deseeded, peeled and sliced
1 lime, cut into wedges

1 Put the rice in a pan, add twice as much water and a pinch of salt and bring to the boil. Turn the heat down and simmer with the lid on for about 25–30 minutes, or until tender and the water has been absorbed, then tip it into a large bowl, fluff up with a fork and let it cool completely.

2 Heat the oil in a large wok. Toss the tofu with the kecap manis, add it to the hot pan and stir-fry on high for a few minutes, or until the tofu begins to turn golden. You may need to add a little more oil as you go. Remove the tofu and leave to one side.

3 Trickle in a little more oil, if needed. Reserve some of the green spring onion/scallion tops to garnish, add the rest to the pan and cook for a minute, then add the garlic and the sambal oelak and cook for a few seconds. Finally add the cold rice and stir it around the pan so every grain is coated in the sauce ingredients. Return the tofu to the pan and stir well, breaking up the rice.

4 Transfer to a serving plate, scatter the reserved chopped spring onions/scallions over the top, then the toasted nuts and sliced papaya. Serve with lime wedges on the side.

Pear, fennel, peas, roasted apple & cobnut salad

I like to add peas to my salads, fresh or frozen they both add little pops of sweetness and you find yourself poking around your bowl wanting more. The two fruits work well as the pear is left raw and fresh and the roasted apple takes on a totally different texture. If you can't get cobnuts, hazelnuts, pecans or almonds would all work well.

Serves 4
Prep: 15 mins Cook: 20 mins

2–3 red eating/dessert apples
juice of 2 lemons
4 ripe dessert pears
1 fennel bulb
1 handful of cobnuts, shelled, or
    nuts of your choice
200g/7oz/1½ cups frozen peas,
    defrosted, or use fresh podded
    if available
1 large handful of rocket/arugula
    leaves

FOR THE DRESSING
6 tbsp extra virgin olive oil
2 tbsp white wine vinegar
juice of ½ lemon
a pinch of sugar (optional)
1 tsp fennel seeds, crushed
1 tsp grainy mustard
1 small handful of dill, finely
    chopped
sea salt and freshly ground black
    pepper

1 Preheat the oven to 200°C/400°F/Gas 6.

2 Core and roughly chop the apples, then toss in some of the lemon juice to prevent discoloration. Core the pears and slice lengthways, then toss in lemon juice. Trim and very finely slice the fennel and toss in lemon juice, reserving any fronds for a garnish.

3 Put the apples and nuts in a roasting pan and bake for about 15–20 minutes until the apples begin to turn golden. Remove and leave to one side.

4 While they are cooking, put the peas in a bowl. Cover with boiling water and leave for 5 minutes, then drain and refresh in cold water.

5 To make the dressing, in a small bowl or jug, whisk together the oil, vinegar and lemon juice, season with salt and pepper, then whisk in the sugar, if using, and stir in the fennel seeds, mustard and dill.

6 Assemble the salad in a large shallow bowl. Add the apples, nuts, pears and fennel and, using your hands, gently tumble together. Drizzle in a little dressing, add the peas and rocket/arugula leaves and again, toss gently to combine. Drizzle over a little more dressing to taste. There may be some left over, and you can put this on the side to serve.

Fig & lentil salad with harissa & mint dressing

This is earthy, sweet, spicy and very satisfying. It uses dried Puy lentils as I love the texture but for ease and speed you could use ready-cooked lentils. If fresh figs aren't available, use dried, roughly chopped and stirred into the lentils. Most supermarkets will stock coconut pieces – you will find them with the prepared snacking fresh fruits.

Serves 4–6
Prep: 15 mins Cook: 40 mins

400g/14oz/2 cups dried Puy lentils,
    rinsed well
a pinch of allspice
2 garlic cloves, grated
about 10 fresh figs
a drizzle of olive oil
200g/7oz coconut pieces
2 celery stalks, trimmed and finely
    sliced
3 spring onions/scallions, trimmed
    and finely chopped
1 large handful of land cress or baby
    spinach leaves
sea salt and freshly ground black
    pepper

FOR THE DRESSING
3 tbsp extra virgin olive oil
1 tbsp white wine vinegar
1–2 tsp harissa, plus extra for
    drizzling
1 handful of mint leaves, finely
    chopped, plus extra to garnish

1 Put the lentils in a pan of salted water and bring to the boil, then turn the heat down and simmer with the lid partially on for about 40 minutes, or until tender. Drain well and leave to one side.

2 While they are cooking, make the dressing. Put the oil and vinegar in a small bowl or jug, whisk and season with salt and pepper, then stir in the harissa and mint. Pour it over the lentils while they are still warm so they soak up the flavours. Add the allspice and garlic and stir well so all the lentils are coated. Taste and season some more if needed.

3 Preheat the oven to 200°C/400°F/Gas 6.

4 Put the figs in a roasting pan and drizzle over the oil, add the coconut to the pan and roast for about 10–15 minutes until the juices start to just run from the figs and the coconut begins to turn golden. When cool enough to handle, slice the coconut pieces into shards and roughly chop the figs or quarter them. Leave to one side.

5 When the lentils are cool, stir in the celery, spring onions/scallions and cress or spinach leaves, then add the figs and half the coconut and stir gently. Transfer to a serving bowl, scatter over the remaining coconut shards and mint leaves and drizzle with a little extra harissa oil from the jar to serve.

For non-vegans...
The Moroccan flavours of this salad work well with lamb kebabs, particularly for a barbecue. Alternatively, crumbled feta would make a tasty topping.

Curried squash with chickpeas and mango

I've been making a variation of this salad for many years now as it is a favourite at home with everyone. It is a vibrant salad layered with wonderful flavour, that can be served alone or with a leafy salad, crusty bread and the yogurt on the side.

Serves 4
Prep: 20 mins Cook: 30 mins

1 butternut squash or pumpkin, halved, deseeded and seeds reserved, peeled and cut into chunky pieces
1 tbsp olive oil
1 tsp dried mint
2 x 400g/14oz cans of chickpeas/garbanzos, drained
2 ripe mangos, pitted, peeled and cut into chunks
1 large handful of almonds, un-skinned
1 handful of coriander/cilantro leaves, chopped
2 baby gem lettuce, trimmed and roughly torn
sea salt and freshly ground black pepper

FOR THE DRESSING
3 tbsp extra virgin olive oil
1 tbsp white wine vinegar
1–2 tsp mild curry powder
1 handful of mint leaves, finely chopped

FOR THE MANGO YOGURT
about 8 tsp soy yogurt
3 tbsp mango chutney
a pinch of mild curry powder

TO SERVE
lime wedges
warm crusty bread

1 Preheat the oven to 200°C/400°F/Gas 6.

2 Put the squash in a large roasting pan, drizzle over the oil, add the dried mint and season well with salt and pepper. Roast for about 20–30 minutes, or until golden and crisp. Remove from the oven and leave to one side.

3 Meanwhile, tip the reserved seeds into a roasting pan and roast in the oven for about 20 minutes until crisp. Leave to one side.

4 Mix together the ingredients for the dressing and season well with salt and pepper. To make the mango yogurt, mix together the yogurt, mango chutney and curry powder.

5 Put the chickpeas/garbanzos in a pan with a little water and heat gently until warm. Drain and transfer to a bowl. Add the squash, mango and almonds and the dressing and toss together carefully, then add half the coriander/cilantro and toss again.

6 To serve, put the lettuce leaves on a plate or a shallow bowl, spoon over the chickpea/garbanzo mixture and scatter with the remaining coriander/cilantro and a few of the roasted seeds. Serve with lime wedges and a little of the mango yogurt on the side and some warm crusty bread.

Roasted ratatouille salad

Making a classic ratatouille is one of those dishes that seems so simple but you can get it so wrong. I was taught that it was better to cook each vegetable individually. Roasting them for a salad seems an easy option and the charred flavours are gorgeous. This is one of those dishes that gets better on standing, so it could sit in the refrigerator for a while, but it needs to be served at room temperature.

Serves 4
Prep: 15 mins Cook: 40 mins

4 red peppers
1–2 tbsp olive oil
4 courgettes/zucchini, roughly
    chopped
2 aubergines/eggplants, roughly
    chopped
2 onions, roughly chopped
a few thyme stalks
about 6 tomatoes, skinned (see
    page 98) and roughly chopped
a few tarragon leaves, chopped
1 handful of black Provençal olives
a drizzle of extra virgin olive oil
a drizzle of balsamic vinegar
1 handful of flatleaf parsley leaves,
    finely chopped
sea salt and freshly ground black
    pepper
warm crusty bread, to serve

1 Preheat the oven to 200°C/400°F/Gas 6.

2 Rub the peppers with a little of the olive oil and place them in a large roasting pan. Put the courgettes/zucchini, aubergines/eggplants, onions and thyme with some salt and pepper in a large bowl, toss together with your hands, then tip them in the roasting pan around the peppers. Roast for about 30–40 minutes, or until the vegetables are charred. Remove, and when the peppers are cool enough to handle, deseed, peel and roughly chop.

3 Put the roasted vegetables in a serving dish, add the tomatoes and tarragon and tumble together. Add the olives and drizzle with the extra virgin olive oil and balsamic vinegar. Season with black pepper and sprinkle the parsley over the top, then serve with warm crusty bread.

Mixed rice with butter beans, griddled courgettes & asparagus with chilli & dill dressing

This is a fabulous jumble of colour, texture and flavour. The rice is lovely and chewy, and adding the dressing while the rice is warm makes sure it absorbs the maximum flavour. This is a good salad to make ahead as the flavours only intensify with a little time.

Serves 4
Prep: 15 mins Cook: 35 mins

300g/10½oz/1¾ cups mixed rice made up of brown basmati, red Camargue and wild rice, rinsed
2 courgettes/zucchini, trimmed and roughly chopped
400g/14oz asparagus spears, trimmed .
a drizzle of olive oil
400g/14oz can of butter/lima beans, drained
1 handful of flatleaf parsley leaves, finely chopped
sea salt and freshly ground black pepper

FOR THE DRESSING
6 tbsp olive oil
2 tbsp raspberry or red wine vinegar
1 handful of dill leaves, finely chopped
1 red chilli, deseeded and finely chopped

1 Put the rice in a pan, add twice as much water and a pinch of salt and bring to the boil. Turn the heat down and simmer with the lid on for about 20–30 minutes, or until tender. Drain well and leave to one side.

2 While the rice is cooking, make the dressing. Whisk together the oil and vinegar and season well with salt and pepper. Add the dill and chilli and mix well. Taste and season some more if needed. Drizzle the dressing over the rice and mix together.

3 Heat a griddle pan to hot. Toss the courgettes/zucchini and asparagus in the oil and season with salt and pepper. Add a few at a time so as not to overcrowd the pan and cook for a few minutes until the underside is charred, then turn and cook the other side until done. Roughly chop the asparagus and add to the rice it along with the courgette/zucchini and butter/lima beans. Give it a stir, then add the parsley and stir once so everything is well blended.

For non-vegans...
Toss in some cubed feta or edam cheese or add some finely chopped anchovies to the salad.

7

SAUCES, DRESSINGS, DIPS & PICKLES

Ranch dressing

This is what you need over your crisp lettuce leaves or some potato skins – it's rich and tangy and hits the spot.

Serves 4–6
Prep: 10 mins

300g/10½oz/1⅓ cups soy yogurt
    with almond or plain soy yogurt
a splash of red wine vinegar
1 garlic clove, finely grated
1 tsp Dijon mustard
a splash of tabasco
1–2 tsp very finely chopped herbs,
    such as tarragon, dill, parsley
    and chives
sea salt and freshly ground black
    pepper

1 Add all the ingredients to a jar with a screw-top lid and shake really well until it is all combined.

2 Open and taste, and season some more if needed, then shake again. Keep tasting until it is just right.

Tahini & date dressing

This is an easy dressing to throw together. It is fairly sweet but really livens up some grains or rice.

Serves 4
Prep: 5 mins

3–4 tbsp tahini
4–5 dates, pitted and roughly
    chopped
juice of ½ lemon
sea salt and freshly ground black
    pepper

1 Add all the ingredients to a food processor along with 100ml/3½fl oz/scant ½ cup of warm water and blitz until smooth, adding more water if needed.

2 Taste and season some more if needed.

Baba ganoush

I think this is superior to hummus – the texture is so palatable and the smoky flavours mingled with tahini and subtle citrus notes are magic. I like to go for one garlic clove and a tablespoon of tahini per aubergine/eggplant. Do use a good peppery extra virgin olive oil for this.

Serves 4–6
Prep: 15 mins Cook: 30 mins

3 aubergines/eggplants
3 plump garlic cloves
1 tbsp olive oil
3 tbsp tahini
juice of 1 lemon
1 handful of parsley leaves
3 tbsp extra virgin olive oil, plus
    extra for drizzling
sea salt and freshly ground black
    pepper
1 handful of pomegranate seeds
    (optional)

1 Preheat the oven to 200°C/400°F/Gas 6.

2 Place the whole aubergines/eggplants and garlic in a roasting pan and rub them all over with the olive oil. Roast for 30 minutes, or until they are tender when poked with a sharp knife. Leave until cool enough to handle, then slash the skin of the aubergines/eggplants and scoop out the flesh, adding it to a food processor. Squeeze the garlic out of the skin and add this also and blitz it to a purée.

3 Add the tahini, lemon juice, parsley and salt and pepper and blitz again. Trickle in the olive oil and press the pulse button to combine, you may not need it all, season with salt and pepper, taste and adjust as it needs it. This can be trial and error with taste – it is like making hummus. Keep tasting and adding more lemon, tahini, or seasoning until it is just right. Spoon it into a serving dish, drizzle over a little extra virgin olive oil and scatter over the pomegranate seeds, if using.

Roasted red pepper hummus

Red pepper hummus is a little lighter and a little sweeter than regular hummus. Kids certainly seem to enjoy it. Remember to keep a watchful eye over the tortillas as they will burn in an instant if you are not careful. You don't want them brown, just golden and crisp. Pictured on previous page.

Makes 450g/1lb
Prep: 15 mins Cook: 1 hour

3 red peppers
½ tbsp olive oil, plus extra for
    finishing and serving
1 x 400g/14oz can of chickpeas/
    garbanzos, drained and juice
    reserved to use in baking (see
    page 16)
2 garlic cloves, roughly chopped
juice of ½ lemon
1 tbsp tahini
3 tsp za'atar
sea salt and freshly ground black
    pepper

TO SERVE
about 6 flour tortillas (most brands
    are vegan)
a drizzle of extra virgin olive oil
a pinch of paprika

1 Preheat the oven to 200°C/400°F/Gas 6.

2 Put the whole peppers in a roasting pan, coat with the olive oil, using your hands, and cook for 45 minutes to 1 hour until the peppers have begun to blacken a little.

3 Remove the peppers from the oven, transfer to a plastic bag or wrap in cling film/plastic wrap and leave until cool enough to handle. Cut away the stalk and seeds and discard, then remove and discard the skin.

4 Put the skinned peppers in a food processor and add the chickpeas/garbanzos, garlic, lemon, tahini and 2 teaspoons of the za'atar. Season well with salt and pepper and blitz until you have a smooth, rich, thick purée. Taste and adjust seasoning as needed or add a little more lemon juice.

5 Slice the tortillas into small triangles, spread them out on two non-stick baking/cookie sheets and sprinkle with paprika. Bake for about 3–5 minutes, or until pale golden.

6 Spoon the hummus into a bowl, sprinkle over the remaining za'atar and a drizzle of olive oil and serve with the tortilla triangles.

For non-vegans...
This hummus would be delicious served with a spiced beef dish or topped with cooked diced lamb.

Piccalilli

In my opinion, piccalilli is the best pickle out there. It needs to have the perfect balance of sharpness with very subtle sweet undertones. The tricky thing when making pickles like this is to know if they taste right, as they really need to sit for a few weeks for the flavours to mingle, but the vegetables should have a 'bite' to them and the sauce should be slightly thickened and be bright yellow from the turmeric. Pictured on page 170.

Makes about 3 jars (2.25kg/ 5lb 8oz)
Prep: 30 mins, plus soaking overnight
Cook: 20 mins

1 cauliflower, cut into florets
2 onions, peeled and roughly chopped
900g/2lb mix of courgettes/zucchini, sliced, runner beans, trimmed and cut into bite-sized pieces, and carrots, sliced
2 tbsp sea salt
2 tbsp plain/all-purpose flour
225g/8oz/1 cup granulated sugar
1 tbsp turmeric
1 tbsp English mustard
1–2 tsp mustard seeds
900ml/31fl oz/3¾ cups pickling vinegar

1 You will need 3 x 750ml/25fl oz/3 cup sterilized sealable jars.

2 Put the cauliflower, onions, courgettes/zucchini, runner beans and carrots in a bowl, sprinkle over the salt and cover with water. Put a plate on top of the vegetables, they need to be submerged, and refrigerate overnight.

3 Drain the vegetables and rinse in cold water. Bring a large pan of water to the boil, add the vegetables and cook for about 2 minutes, then drain and refresh in cold water. They need to have plenty of crunch.

4 Mix together the flour, sugar, turmeric, mustard and mustard seeds, then add a little vinegar and mix into a paste. Pour the remaining vinegar into a pan and stir in the paste. Bring to the boil, stirring continuously, then turn the heat down and simmer for about 15 minutes. Remove from the heat, add the vegetables and stir to coat. Divide the mixture between the sterilized jars and seal. Store for at least 1 month before using. Once open, keep the jar of picalilli in the refrigerator.

Green bean salsa

A great condiment to spoon onto salads, sandwiches, tortillas or some of the all-in-one roasts in this book. Go easy with the lime at first, then add more a little at a time until the taste makes you happy! Make it hot or not with the chilli. Pictured overleaf.

Serves 4–6
Prep: 10 mins Cook: 10 mins

300g/10½oz fine green beans, trimmed and chopped into bite-sized pieces
1 green chilli, deseeded and finely chopped (optional)
1 handful of dill fronds, finely chopped
½ tsp caraway seeds
½ tsp caster/superfine sugar
juice of 1–2 limes
1–2 tbsp red wine vinegar
about 3 tbsp extra virgin olive oil
sea salt and freshly ground black pepper

1 Bring a pan of salted water to the boil, add the green beans and bring to the boil, then turn the heat down and simmer for about 5 minutes, or until just tender but still with a bit of a bite. Drain well and refresh in cold water to stop the cooking process.

2 In a bowl, mix the chilli, if using, dill, caraway seeds, sugar, lime juice, vinegar and oil and season well with salt and pepper. Taste and adjust with more salt, lime juice or sugar.

Red cabbage sauerkraut

If you've got a jar of this in the refrigerator you will soon be spooning it on to everything. It's addictive as it adds that tang and sharpness that you just sometimes need. It's also an easy way of eating raw and it is good for the gut. It can hardly be called fast food – you have to wait a few days for it to do its thing – so it's good to make it in bulk, then you will always have a jar ready to dip into when the craving strikes! Pictured overleaf.

Makes 1 x 1 litre/35fl oz/4⅓ cup jar
Prep: 20 mins, plus fermentation
 time (about 3–14 days)

2kg/4lb 8 oz red cabbage, halved,
 trimmed and finely shredded
1 tbsp sea salt
1 tsp caraway seeds, fennel seeds,
 juniper berries or fresh chopped
 ginger

1 You will need a 1 litre/35fl oz/4⅓ cup sterilized sealable jar.

2 Tip all the cabbage, salt and herbs into a large non-metallic bowl – glass is best. Using your hands, toss it all together.

3 Using a pestle or the edge of a rolling pin, start to pound the cabbage. It will begin to squash down and very soon it will start to release its water. Keep going with this for about 10 minutes, or until there is enough water in the bowl to cover the cabbage.

4 Pack the cabbage into the sterilized jar a little at a time, pushing and pressing it firmly down after each addition so the cabbage is immersed under water. Make sure the top layer is under water, then seal the lid. Leave for 3–14 days on the kitchen worktop to ferment and get to the required taste you like – the longer you leave it the stronger it will become. It will keep for weeks in the refrigerator once opened.

Satay sauce

I adore peanut sauce. You could serve it with the Vegetable Kebabs (see page 72), some skewered tofu or just add a dollop to liven up a rice dish. I've made this over the years with ground peanuts and peanut butter and they are both really tasty.

Serves 6–8
Prep: 10 mins Cook: 10 mins

400ml/14fl oz can of coconut milk
2–3 tbsp chunky peanut butter
1 tbsp demerara/turbinado sugar
a pinch of chilli flakes (add more or
    less to your heat preference)
juice of 1 lime
sea salt and freshly ground black
    pepper

1 Put all the ingredients in a pan and bring to the boil, then turn the heat down and simmer, stirring continuously, for about 10 minutes until it thickens. Taste and season if needed, adding more lime juice, salt or sugar. Spoon it into a serving bowl for dipping or spooning!

Vegan mayonnaise

This is super-tangy and delicious mayo uses the clever chickpea/garbanzo juice, aquafaba (see page 16), which amalgamates with the vinegar, mustard and oil to make a creamy version of mayonnaise. Turn it into a seafood-flavoured cocktail sauce for a salad by stirring in some ketchup.

Makes about 200ml/7fl oz/
**   scant 1 cup**
Prep: 15 mins

4 tbsp aquafaba (see page 16)
¼ tsp cream of tartar
1 tbsp lemon juice
2 tsp white wine vinegar
½–1 tbsp maple syrup
¼ tsp English mustard
about 150ml/5fl oz/scant ⅔ cup
    rapeseed oil or sunflower oil
sea salt and freshly ground black
    pepper

1 Put the aquafaba, cream of tartar, lemon juice and vinegar in the bowl of a food mixer and whisk for 1 minute until it is all blended. Then whisk in the maple syrup and mustard.

2 With the mixer on low, drizzle in the oil a little at time until it becomes thick and creamy, about 10 minutes. You may need a little more oil for the right consistency. Season with salt and pepper, mix and taste. Adjust as needed, adding more mustard or vinegar. Spoon into a bowl, cover and keep in the refrigerator for up to 3 days.

Kimchi

Ready-made kimchi often contains shrimp paste, so I make my own. A quantity this size will last me all year, as you only need a little to transform your food. Chilli paste is best bought from an Asian store, and I buy a Korean one called Hot Pepper Paste, or use Korean red pepper powder (*gochugaru* – see page 14). If you tell your Asian supermarket that you wish to make kimchi, they will point out the right paste – mine actually gave me the recipe.

Makes 2 x 1 litre/35fl oz/4⅓ cup jars
Prep: 30 mins, plus fermentation

2 Chinese nappa cabbages, trimmed and leaves sliced lengthways
3 tbsp sea salt
2 bunches of spring onions/ scallions, trimmed and finely chopped
4 garlic cloves, finely chopped
5cm/2in piece of fresh root ginger, peeled and grated
2–3 tsp caster/superfine sugar
1 apple, peeled, cored and grated
3 tbsp hot chilli paste

1 You will need two 1 litre/35fl oz/4⅓ cup sterilized sealable jars.

2 To make the kimchi, put the cabbage in a large bowl, sprinkle over the salt and toss it together so all the leaves are coated. Now pour over enough cold water to cover, and leave it to sit for a couple of hours, making sure the cabbage is immersed in the salty water.

3 Drain well and pat the leaves dry with a dish towel (the lady in our local Asian store told me to peg them on the washing line to dry in the sun – it's your call!). Put the spring onions/scallions, garlic, ginger, sugar, apple and chilli paste in a large bowl and stir well. Begin to add the cabbage leaves a few at a time and use your hands to turn and coat them in the paste.

4 Pack the leaves into the prepared jars, pressing down firmly as you do. Liquid will be released and the leaves all need to be submerged under this. Put the lid on, seal and leave at room temperature for at least a week for it to ferment. The longer you leave it, the stronger in taste it will become. Once open, keep it in the refrigerator.

8

DESSERTS

Griddled pineapple in rum & orange blossom syrup with pistachio & coconut cream

This is one of those desserts that is effortless to execute but guarantees a wow at the table! You are going to have to go full-fat here as the lower-calorie coconut milks just don't whip up the same. Choose a coconut cream that is rich and creamy with a high percentage of coconut extract – the cream separates better and has a thicker layer at the top. It also separates more if cold so put it in the refrigerator before using.

Serves 4
Prep: 20 mins Cook: 15 mins

2 large pineapples, outer skin removed and flesh sliced into 1.5cm/⅝ in rounds
4 tbsp dark rum
1 tbsp orange blossom water
1 tbsp maple syrup
1 handful of pistachio nuts, roughly chopped
1 handful of pomegranate seeds

FOR THE COCONUT CREAM
400ml/14fl oz can of good-quality full-fat coconut milk, refrigerator cold
a drizzle of maple syrup

1 Put the pineapple pieces in a shallow dish. Mix the rum, orange blossom water and maple syrup together, and pour it over the pineapple, turning to coat. Leave to one side while you make the cream.

2 Skim off the thick coconut cream at the top of the can, put it into the bowl of a food mixer and beat for a minute or so until thick. If it needs thinning down at all, add a little of the coconut water from the can. Spoon it out into a dish and drizzle over the maple syrup.

3 Heat a griddle pan to hot, add the pineapple slices a few at time, shaking off the juice, and cook for about a minute each side until golden and char-lined. Repeat with the remaining slices. Tip the remaining juice into a small pan and heat gently. If you need more, top up with a little more rum and orange blossom water. Bring to a bubble and cook for few minutes.

4 To serve, transfer a few pineapple pieces to each plate, drizzle over the syrup, scatter over the pistachio nuts and pomegranate seeds and serve with a dollop of coconut cream.

Pear & raspberry tart with pistachio frangipane

This is a great dinner-party showpiece as it both tastes and looks gorgeous. Pear and raspberry work so well together, the raspberries adding the necessary tartness to offset the sweetness of the pear. This is excellent unadorned but a trickle of dairy-free cream would be a nice addition. Use a light hand with the pastry for a deliciously crisp and flaky result.

Serves 8
Prep: 20 mins, plus chilling
Cook: 1 hour

225g/8oz/heaped 1¾ cups plain/all-purpose flour, plus extra for dusting
a pinch of salt
125g/4oz/½ cup dairy-free spread, plus extra for greasing
2 dessert pears, peeled, cored and quartered lengthways
150g/5oz/1 cup fresh raspberries, any large ones halved
small handful of pistachio nuts, chopped
icing/confectioners' sugar, for dusting

FOR THE FRANGIPANE
200ml/7fl oz/scant 1 cup aquafaba (juice from canned chickpeas/garbanzos, see page 16)
150g/5oz/⅔ cup dairy-free spread
150g/5oz/scant 1 cup golden caster/superfine sugar
100g/3½oz/⅔ cup pistachio nuts, finely ground
150g/5oz/1½ cups ground almonds
1 tbsp plain/all-purpose flour

1 Preheat the oven to 200°C/400°F/Gas 6 and grease a rectangular, loose-bottomed tart pan about 13 x 36cm/5 x 14in or a 23cm/9in round pan with dairy-free spread.

2 To make the pastry, put the flour, salt and dairy-free spread in a large bowl and rub together until it resembles breadcrumbs. Add 2 teaspoons of cold water and work to a dough. Form into a ball and flatten, wrap in cling film/plastic wrap and put in the refrigerator to rest for 20 minutes.

3 Roll out the pastry on a lightly floured board so it is slightly larger than the tart pan, then transfer it to the pan, pressing it into the base and letting it overlap the sides. Fill with parchment paper and baking beans. Bake for 15 minutes, then remove the beans and paper and return to the oven for 3 minutes to crisp up. Trim the edges to neaten and set aside. Turn the oven down to 180°C/350°F/Gas 4.

4 For the frangipane, put the aquafaba in a small saucepan, bring to the boil and simmer for about 5 minutes until slightly reduced. Set aside to cool. Add the dairy-free spread and sugar to the bowl of a food mixer and beat for 5 minutes until creamy. Add the pistachios and almonds, the cooled aquafaba and flour and mix until combined.

5 Add half the raspberries to the frangipane and stir them in gently, then spoon into the pastry base being careful not to over-fill. Press in the pears, then scatter in the remaining raspberries, pushing them into the frangipane. Bake for 40 minutes, until golden. The top will still be wobbly, but will set as it cools. Leave to cool in the pan before releasing. Transfer to a serving plate or board, scatter over the remaining pistachio nuts and dust with icing/confectioners' sugar.

Poached peaches with maple yogurt

Simple, fresh and aromatic – the cardamom adds just that little extra *je ne sais quoi*. You can make these ahead and let them cool, in which case the flavours intensify. Put them in the refrigerator but serve at room temperature. Or you can serve them warm from the pan.

Serves 4
Prep: 5 mins Cook: 15 mins

8 peaches (not too ripe)
seeds from 5 cardamom pods,
    crushed
1 vanilla pod/bean, sliced
    lengthways
about 2–3 tbsp caster/superfine
    sugar

FOR THE MAPLE YOGURT
300g/10½oz/scant 1¼ cups soy
    yogurt
2–3 tbsp maple syrup

1 Put the peaches in large pan with the cardamom, vanilla pod, sugar and about 1 litre/35fl oz/4⅓ cups of water. Bring to the boil, then turn the heat down to a simmer. Put a round of parchment paper over the peaches and place a plate on top to weigh it down so the peaches stay submerged under the water. Simmer very gently to poach them for about 10–15 minutes until soft.

2 Remove the peaches with a slotted spoon and leave to one side. Pour a little of the poaching water into a small pan, add the vanilla pod, bring to the boil and cook for a few minutes until it begins to thicken slightly. Spoon it over the peaches.

3 To make the maple yogurt, mix together the yogurt and maple syrup. Transfer the peaches into serving bowls and spoon over the yogurt to serve.

Roasted cassis plums with cashew cream

This type of dessert appeals to me as it is low maintenance. Also, where I live in the countryside there are so many plum trees along walkways and fields and nobody seems to pick them, they just drop to the floor and waste. So I lay my hands on as many as I can when in season and turn them into sauces or jams, put them in crumbles or roast for a dessert when time is limited. If you make plenty of the cashew cream, it will keep in the refrigerator for up to a week.

Serves 4
Prep: 15 mins Cook: 30 mins

400g/14oz Victoria plums, washed,
    halved or quartered and pitted
a sprinkle of caster/superfine sugar
    (depending on how sweet the
    plums are, you many only need
    the tiniest amount)
3½ tbsp cassis or apple juice

FOR THE CASHEW CREAM
150g/5oz/1¼ cups cashew nuts,
    soaked overnight
1 tsp vanilla extract

1 Preheat the oven to 190°C/375°F/Gas 5 and line a roasting pan with parchment paper.

2 Put the plums, sugar and cassis or apple juice in a bowl and toss together to coat, then tip into the prepared roasting pan and spread them out. Roast for 20–30 minutes, giving them a stir halfway through.

3 While they are cooking, make the cashew cream.
Drain the cashews, then put them in a food processor with about 5 tablespoons of water and the vanilla and blitz to a paste, adding a little more water and continuing to whiz until it reaches your desired consistency.

4 Divide the plums up between serving bowls and serve with the cream on the side.

Pink grapefruit sorbet with a drizzle of gin

The gin is optional, of course, but it is fun to have an alcoholic dessert occasionally and it does soak in rather nicely. You can cheat and buy a carton of freshly squeezed pink grapefruit juice as long as it is pure and doesn't contain any concentrates.

Serves 4
Prep: 15 mins, plus churning and freezing

500ml/17fl oz/generous 2 cups freshly squeezed pink grapefruit juice
juice of 1 lemon
120g/3½oz/heaped ⅔ cup caster/ superfine sugar
your favourite gin, to drizzle
lime wedges, to serve
a few mint leaves, for decoration

1 Put half the grapefruit juice, the lemon juice and sugar in a pan over a low heat until it is warmed and the sugar dissolves. Remove from the heat, then stir in the remaining juice and let it cool completely.

2 Pour it into an ice cream maker and churn for 40 minutes or as per the manufacturer's instructions. Scoop it into a freezerproof container and put in the freezer until frozen and ready to serve. If you don't have an ice cream maker you will need to freeze the sorbet for a couple of hours until it begins to freeze around the edges. Return it to a mixer and mix, or crush with a fork, then freeze again. You will need to do this about three times to stop any large ice crystals forming.

3 Scoop the sorbet into bowls, drizzle over a measure of gin, if using, and decorate with a lime wedge. This is best eaten pretty soon after freezing as the flavours deplete with time. Serve decorated with mint leaves.

Basil, lime & mandarin sorbet

These flavours are inspired by my favourite perfume; they go together perfectly for a light, refreshing and mouth-tingling dessert. This is nice to serve for a change from a creamy ice cream, especially if you've eaten a lot. It's much lower in fat, too, which means you can eat more of it! This is best eaten within a week of being made.

Serves 4
Prep: 15 mins, plus churning and freezing
Cook: 5 mins

juice from about 4 mandarin oranges or use regular orange juice (about 100ml/3½fl oz/scant ½ cup juice)
zest of 3 limes and juice of 8 (about 200ml/7fl oz/scant 1 cup juice)
250–300g/9–12oz/1–1¼ cups caster/superfine sugar (depending on how sweet the oranges are)
1 handful of fresh basil leaves, torn, plus whole leaves, to garnish

1 Put the mandarin juice, lime zest and sugar in a pan with 300ml/10½fl oz/1¼ cups of water, bring to a simmer and heat until the sugar has dissolved.

2 Remove from the heat, stir in the lime juice and add the basil leaves, pushing them down into the syrup. Leave to cool completely, taste and add more juice if needed. Pass through a sieve/fine-mesh strainer, then pour into an ice cream maker and churn according to the manufacturer's instructions. Transfer to a freezerproof container and put in the freezer until frozen and ready to serve. If you don't have an ice cream maker you will need to freeze the sorbet for a couple of hours until it begins to freeze around the edges. Return it to a mixer and mix or crush with a fork, then freeze again. You will need to do this about three times to stop any large ice crystals forming.

3 Scoop into serving bowls and decorate with basil leaves to serve.

Summer pudding with rose water & bay

This has only a subtle flavour of rose water and bay running through it – it is a pudding of pure summertime, but there is nothing stopping you making it in the winter using frozen berries. They do need to be juicy, though, so they will burst and flood the bread with colour. I think this is best made with standard white sliced bread rather than anything fancy.

Serves 6
Prep: 20 mins, plus chilling
       overnight
Cook: 5 mins

700g/1lb 9oz mixed berries, such
     as strawberries, raspberries,
     blackberries, red currants (reserve
     a few for the top)
2 tsp rose water
1 bay leaf, torn at edges to release
     the flavour
about 1–2 tsp caster/superfine sugar
     (depending on how sweet the
     fruit is)
about 7–8 slices of medium white
     sliced bread, crusts removed
icing/confectioners' sugar, for dusting
soy yogurt, to serve

1 You will need a medium-sized pudding basin – approx 900ml/31fl oz/3⅔ cups – lined with cling film/plastic wrap to help to remove the pudding easily.

2 Put the fruit in a pan with the rose water, bay, sugar and 1 tablespoon of water – you may need to add a little more while it cooks. Heat gently for a few minutes until the fruit softens, but don't let it turn to mush. Remove from the heat and let it cool completely.

3 Line the pudding basin. Remember, the neater you line it the neater it will look when it is turned out of the bowl. Cut a round of bread for the base of the bowl and save a slice to cut out a round for the top. Slice the remaining bread into even fingers, lengthways. Push the round of bread into the bottom of the bowl then line the fingers of bread the whole way round, overlapping them as you go.

4 When the fruit has cooled, remove the bay and spoon the fruit and any juice into the bowl to fill. Cut out a round of bread large enough for the top, put this on top of the fruit and press it down firmly. Put a small plate on top and put a can on top so that the pudding is squashed down and becomes compact. Put in the refrigerator overnight to chill.

5 When ready to serve, carefully insert a palette knife/metal spatula around the edge of the bowl to release it and invert it onto a serving plate. Remove the cling film/plastic wrap. Decorate the top with remaining berries and dust with icing/confectioners' sugar. Slice to serve with a dollop of soy yogurt.

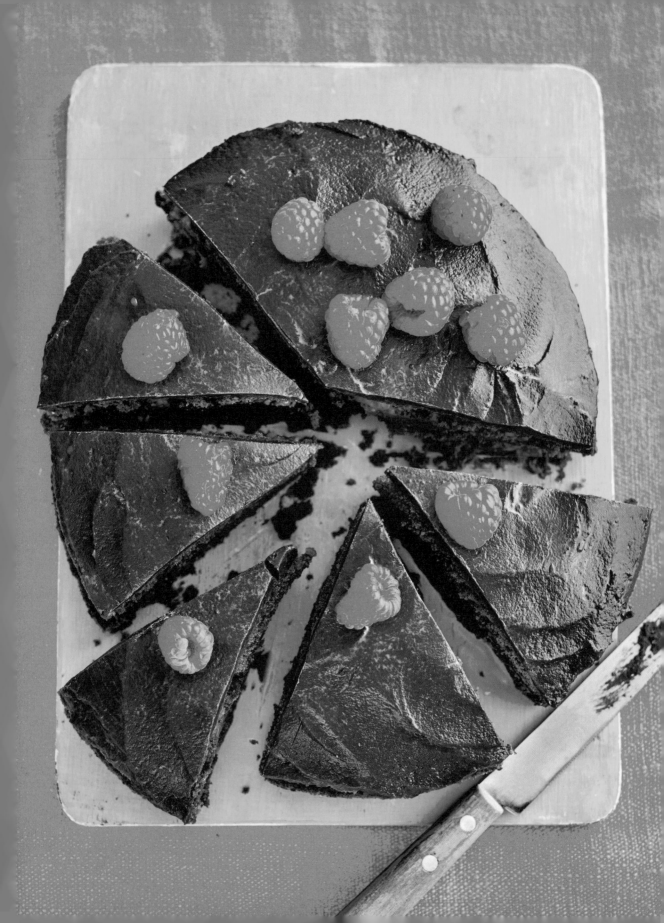

Decadent chocolate & raspberry cake

The best bit about this cake is that you can lick the spoon knowing there is no raw egg involved. Don't expect the same rise you would get for a cake with eggs – but it will still look the part once sandwiched together and piled with chocolate frosting.

Serves 8
Prep: 15 mins   Cook: 30 mins

85g/3oz/scant ⅓ cup dairy-free
    spread
2 tbsp maple syrup
1 tsp apple cider vinegar
300g/10½oz/2½ cups self-raising/
    self-rising flour
2 tbsp dairy-free cocoa/unsweetened
    chocolate powder, at least 70%
    cocoa, plus extra for dusting
100g/3½ oz/½ cup golden caster/
    superfine sugar
1 tsp bicarbonate of soda/baking
    soda
½ vanilla pod, seeds only
300g/10½oz fresh raspberries,
    roughly chopped, leave some
    whole for topping

FOR THE CHOCOLATE FROSTING
200g/7oz dairy-free dark chocolate,
    at least 70% cocoa
80g/3oz dairy-free spread
2 tbsp almond milk or dairy-free
    milk of your choice
6–8 tbsp icing/confectioners'
    sugar, sifted plus a dusting for
    decoration if you wish

1 Preheat the oven to 180°C/350°F/Gas 4 and base-line two 20cm/8in cake pans with parchment paper.

2 Put the dairy-free spread in the bowl of a food mixer, add the maple syrup, apple cider vinegar and 300ml/10½fl oz/ 1¼ cups of boiling water. Mix slowly until the spread has melted and everything is combined.

3 In another bowl, put the flour, cocoa, sugar, bicarbonate of soda/baking soda and the vanilla seeds and stir. Add this to the wet mixture and beat on slow until you have a smooth batter.

4 Divide the mixture between the pans, smooth the top and bake for about 20–30 minutes (check after 20 minutes), or until a skewer poked into the middle comes out clean.

5 Leave the cakes to cool in the pans for 10 minutes, then invert onto a wire rack to cool completely.

6 To make the frosting, put the chocolate and dairy-free spread in a heatproof bowl. Sit it over a pan of just simmering water and stir occasionally until melted. Remove from the heat and leave to cool a little, then stir in the milk and slowly add the icing/confectioners' sugar, beating as you go, until it begins to thicken and become glossy. Put in the refrigerator to set.

7 To assemble the cake, remove the frosting from the refrigerator and beat until glossy. Spread generously over one of the sponges, top with most of the raspberries then top with the other sponge and cover with the remaining frosting, and use a knife to neaten. Top with the remaining raspberries and a dusting of icing/confectioners' sugar or cocoa, if using.

Orange, marmalade & almond cake

This is more like a pudding than a traditional cake – it is super-moist with lots of flavour, tangy with almonds and is delicious served with a dollop of soy yogurt.

Serves 8–10
Prep: 15 mins Cook: 50 mins

100ml/3½fl oz/scant ½ cup
  sunflower oil
100g/3½oz/1 cup caster/superfine
  sugar
 2 tbsp marmalade
200g/7 oz/scant 1⅔ cups plain/
  all-purpose flour, sifted
2 tsp baking powder, sifted
40g/1½oz/scant ½ cup ground
  almonds
2 oranges, peel, pith and pips
  removed and flesh chopped
200g/14fl oz/2 cups plain soy
  yogurt or soy yogurt with almond
6 tbsp aquafaba (juice from
  canned chickpeas/garbanzos,
  see page 16)

FOR THE TOPPING
1 orange, peeled with a zester into
  fine strips, and juice of ½ orange
2 tsp caster/superfine sugar
icing/confectioners' sugar, sifted, for
  dusting

1 Preheat the oven to 180°C/350°F/Gas 4 and line a 20cm/8in, deep, loose-bottomed cake pan with parchment paper.

2 Put the oil and sugar in the bowl of a food mixer and beat until combined, then beat in the marmalade and gradually tip in the flour and baking powder and beat slowly until combined. Stir in the almonds, oranges, soy yogurt and aquafaba and beat gently until combined. Spoon into the prepared pan.

3 Bake for about 50 minutes until risen and golden and a skewer inserted in the middle comes out clean.

4 While the cake is baking, make the topping. Put the orange zest and juice and sugar in a pan with 1 tablespoon of water and heat for about 10 minutes until it starts to caramelize, stirring occasionally so it doesn't burn.

5 Leave the cake to cool for 10 minutes, then release from the pan and leave to cool on a wire rack. Dust with icing/confectioners' sugar, then spoon over the orange zest topping and any remaining juice to serve.

Rhubarb & liquorice pudding

This is basically a fruit bottom with a sponge top, baked to deliciousness. It's so good hot, served with vegan custard, coconut ice cream or soy yogurt. Bird's custard is vegan so make it as per the packet instructions with sugar and a dairy-free milk of your choice. You could prepare the fruit the night before, the flavour of the liquorice will come through stronger the longer it is left, but you should remove it before baking.

Serves 4
Prep: 20 mins Cook: 35 mins

400g/12oz rhubarb, trimmed and
  chopped into 3cm/1¼in pieces
1 stick liquorice root, broken in half
1 tbsp soft light brown sugar
1 cooking apple, peeled, cored and
  roughly chopped
icing/confectioners' sugar, sifted, for
  dusting
custard, soy yogurt or ice cream, to
  serve

FOR THE SPONGE TOPPING
125g/4oz sunflower spread
125g/4oz/heaped ⅔ cup soft light
  brown sugar
6 tbsp aquafaba (juice from
  canned chickpeas/garbanzos,
  see page 16)
125g/4oz/1 cup self-raising/self-
  rising flour

1 Preheat the oven to 180°C/350°F/Gas 4.

2 First prepare the fruit. Put the rhubarb, liquorice root, sugar and apple in a pan with a trickle of water. Simmer gently for about 5 minutes until the rhubarb is tender, then remove from the heat and leave to cool. Spoon it into a deep ovenproof baking dish.

3 To make the sponge topping, put the sunflower spread and sugar in the bowl of a food mixer and mix using the beaters for about 10 minutes until pale and creamy, then slowly drizzle in the aquafaba along with a tablespoon of flour. When it is all combined, fold in the remaining flour.

4 Pour the sponge batter over the fruit and spread it out to cover. Bake for 30–35 minutes, or until a skewer comes out clean when inserted into the middle. Dust with icing/confectioners' sugar to serve with custard, soy yogurt or ice cream.

Roasted black cherries with marzipan, coconut cream & vanilla ice cream

This ice cream requires a good thick coconut cream to make it really creamy. The sweet and succulent cherries burst and take on the flavour of the cassis. Most cassis liqueurs are vegan, but do check the label.

Serves 4
Prep: 30 mins, plus churning and freezing
Cook: 20 mins

400g/14oz fresh black cherries, pitted
1 tbsp demerara/turbinado sugar
2–3 tbsp cassis liqueur
200g/7oz almond paste, grated

FOR THE ICE CREAM
2 x 400ml/14fl oz cans of full-fat coconut cream
150g/5oz/¾ cup golden caster/superfine sugar
1 vanilla pod/bean, sliced lengthways and seeds removed
2 tsp cornflour/cornstarch

1 First, make the ice cream. Pour 1½ cans of coconut cream into a pan with the sugar and vanilla pod and gently warm but do not bring to the boil.

2 Beat the remaining coconut cream with the cornflour/cornstarch until smooth, then pour it into the pan, stir and simmer for 5–6 minutes until it begins to thicken. Keep stirring it so it remains lump-free but don't let it boil.

3 Leave the ice cream mixture to cool completely, then remove the vanilla pod. Pour it into an ice cream maker and churn for about 45 minutes until creamy and frozen or follow the manufacturer's instructions. Pour into a freezerproof container, cover and put in the freezer until ready to serve. If you haven't got an ice cream maker, pour the mixture into a flat freezerproof container and put in the freezer for a couple of hours, then remove and add it to a food processor and whiz or break up with a fork. Put it back in the freezer and repeat twice more once frozen. This is to stop large ice crystals forming.

4 Preheat the oven to 190°C/375°F/Gas 5.

5 Tip the cherries into a roasting pan, toss with the sugar and bake for about 6 minutes until the cherries start to burst. Pour the cassis over the top and sprinkle with the almond paste. Put in the oven for a further 5–6 minutes, or until the marzipan is golden. Remove and divide up between bowls and serve while hot with a scoop of ice cream.

Apple & blackberry pie

Everyone needs an easy fruit pie recipe and you can adjust your fruit according to the seasons: apple, strawberry and vanilla; pear and walnut; plum and cinnamon, or apricot and almond. I don't like to stew my fruit first as I think it cooks perfectly in the pie, but you can cook it first for a few minutes if you wish.

Serves 4
Prep: 20 mins Cook: 45 mins

300g/10½oz fresh blackberries or use frozen, defrosted
2 cooking apples, peeled, cored and roughly chopped (leave fairly big) tossed in 1 tbsp demerara/turbinado sugar
2 star anise
zest of ½ lemon
1 tbsp dairy-free milk, soy or almond
a sprinkling of caster/superfine sugar

FOR THE PASTRY
225g/8oz/heaped 1¾ cups plain/all-purpose flour, plus extra for dusting
a pinch of salt
125g/4oz sunflower spread, refrigerator cold, plus extra for greasing

1 Preheat the oven to 200°C/400°F/Gas 6 and grease a 20cm/8in pie pan.

2 First make the pastry. Put the flour and salt in a bowl and mix, then add the sunflower spread and rub it in using your fingertips until it resembles breadcrumbs. Trickle in a sprinkling of ice cold water, then bring the mixture together with your hands until it forms a dough. Turn it out onto a floured board, knead gently and flatten, then divide in half.

3 Roll one half of the pastry out 5cm/2in larger than the pie pan, then line the pan with it, letting the edges drape over the sides. Line with parchment paper and baking beans and bake for about 10 minutes (this is just to make sure you don't get a soggy bottom). Remove the pan from the oven, remove the beans and paper and pile in the fruit, star anise and lemon zest. Roll out the remaining pastry and lay it over the top of the fruit. Push the edges down, trim and crimp them together. Brush over the soy or almond milk, then sprinkle with sugar and bake for about 30–35 minutes, or until the pastry is golden and crisp.

Slow-baked vanilla rice pudding

This is a crowd pleaser pud, as it's really nostalgic. It requires few ingredients and minimum effort, just a slow bake. You need much less rice than you think as it quadruples in size whilst cooking. I like it with just a subtle taste of nutmeg but finely grated lemon or orange zest would work and, if feeding the kids, a grating of chocolate always goes down well!

Serves 4–6
Prep: 10 mins Cook: 2 hours

2 tbsp sunflower spread
150g/5oz/⅔ cup short-grain/
    pudding rice, rinsed
700ml/24fl oz/3 cups almond milk,
    plus extra for topping up
250ml/9fl oz/generous 1 cup
    coconut milk drink
1 vanilla pod/bean, split lengthways
50g/2oz/⅓ cup golden caster/
    superfine sugar
a pinch of freshly grated nutmeg

1 Preheat the oven to 150°C/300°F/Gas 2 and lightly grease a large shallow ovenproof dish with a little of the sunflower spread.

2 Put the rice, milks, vanilla pod/bean and sugar in a pan, stir and bring to the boil, then simmer for a few minutes.

3 Transfer the mixture into the prepared dish, top with the remaining sunflower spread and sprinkle with the nutmeg. Cover with foil and put in the oven for about 40–50 minutes, then check on it, give it a stir and top up with a little more almond milk, if needed. Put the foil back on and cook for another 40–50 minutes, check and stir again, adding milk if it is too dry, then remove the foil and cook for about 20 minutes until it is creamy, the rice is tender and it is golden on top.

Peach & raspberry whisky trifle

I used to work in a vegetarian restaurant that served the most wonderful trifles, and I have been hooked ever since. I like to make double the amount of cake you need and freeze half for later, but if you don't wish to have any cake left over, just halve the sponge recipe.

Serves 6–8
Prep: 20 mins, plus setting
Cook: 35 mins

1–2 tbsp strawberry jam
1–2 tbsp whisky or sherry (optional)
300g/10½oz raspberries, halved
3–4 peaches, pitted and sliced
400g/14fl oz can coconut milk
50g/2oz dairy-free dark chocolate
a few pistachio nuts, chopped
icing/confectioners' sugar, to dust

FOR THE SPONGE BASE
400ml/14fl oz/1⅔ cups almond
  milk
2 tbsp golden/light corn syrup
1 tsp vanilla extract
120ml/4fl oz/½ cup rapeseed oil
400g/14oz/3¼ cups self-raising/
  self-rising flour, sifted
1¼ tsp bicarbonate of soda/baking
  soda, sifted
1 tsp baking powder, sifted
225g/8oz/1 cup caster/superfine
  sugar

FOR THE CUSTARD
1 tbsp cornflour/cornstarch
500ml/17fl oz/2 cups almond milk
1 tbsp golden caster/superfine sugar
1–2 tsp vanilla extract
a pinch of turmeric (just for colour)

FOR THE JELLY
150ml/5fl oz/⅔ cup orange juice
2g agar agar

1 Preheat the oven to 180°C/350°C/Gas 4 and line two 20cm/8in loose-bottomed cake pans with parchment paper.

2 To make the sponge, put the milk, golden syrup, vanilla extract and oil into the bowl of a food mixer and beat to combine, then gradually sift over the flour, bicarbonate of soda/baking soda, baking powder and sugar and beat until it is all creamed together. Pour into the pans and bake for 30 minutes until pale golden and risen. Cool for 5 minutes, then turn onto a wire rack and leave to cool completely.

3 For the custard, mix the cornflour/cornstarch and a splash of milk to a paste. Pour the remaining milk, sugar and vanilla into a pan and heat gently, stir in the cornflour/cornstarch mix and stir continuously as it thickens. Whisk in the turmeric and top up with more milk if needed. Set aside.

4 Spread one of the cakes with jam and break into pieces (you won't need both cakes), then put it in the bottom of a large glass serving bowl. Pour over the whisky or sherry, if using, and add a large handful of raspberries.

5 To make the jelly, put the juice and the agar agar in a pan, bring to the boil for 2 minutes, whisking as you go, then remove from the heat. Cool slightly then pour over the fruit and sponge. Put it in the fridge to set for a couple of hours.

6 To assemble, layer the remaining raspberries, peaches and custard over the jelly base, finishing with custard. Spoon off the thick top layer in the can of coconut milk and whisk until thickened. Spoon it over the trifle, then grate over the chocolate and decorate with more raspberries and pistachio nuts, if using, and a light dusting of icing/confectioners' sugar. Put back in the refrigerator until ready to serve.

Mixed berry pavlova

This is a revelation: making meringue with the liquid from canned chickpeas/garbanzos. Known as aquafaba, it has emulsifying, foaming, binding, gelatinizing and thickening properties – wow! It whisks up for meringues just like egg whites, although it isn't as stable as meringue once cooked, so be aware that it is fragile. I didn't use a nut cream with this as it is not light enough to sit on the meringue without it breaking. Instead, the pavlova tastes great with soy yogurt, or just piled high with fruit and a drizzle of dairy-free single cream.

Serves 4–6
Prep: 20 mins Cook: 2½ hours

200ml/7fl oz/scant 1 cup aquafaba (juice from canned chickpeas/garbanzos, see page 16)
125g/4oz/½ cup caster/superfine sugar
¼ tsp cream of tartar
1 large handful of mixed berries of your choice, frozen and defrosted or fresh
5–6 tbsp soy yogurt
a few edible flowers for decoration (optional)
a dusting of icing/confectioners' sugar, to serve

1 Preheat the oven to 110°C/225°F/Gas ¼, line a baking/cookie sheet with parchment paper and draw out a circle on the paper about 24cm/9½in in diameter.

2 In the bowl of a food mixer or using a bowl and a hand-held whisk, add the aquafaba and whisk until it forms soft peaks, which may take anything from 3–6 minutes. Slowly tip in the sugar and cream of tartar, whisking as you go, until it forms stiff peaks. You should be able to hold the bowl over your head without fear!

3 Carefully spoon the meringue on the prepared sheet, spreading it around to fill the circle, then use a dessert spoon and make dollops all around the edge. This is to make the sides a little higher than the middle.

4 Bake for 2½ hours, remove from the oven and cool completely. It may be tricky to remove from the paper as it will be delicate. If it is easier, cut around the paper and transfer it all to a serving plate. Spoon the soy yogurt on to the meringue. Top with berries and edible flowers, if using, dust with icing/confectioners' sugar and slice to serve.

9

SWEET TREATS

St Clement's shortbread

Shortbread is all about the buttery taste so using a butter substitute can be tricky, but the addition of lemon and orange zest give this that essential zing and it is perfectly crumbly shortbread. A light touch and cool hands is required with shortbread, as with making pastry. For an extra indulgence, you could top the shortbread with melted dairy-free dark chocolate.

Makes 12 slices
Prep: 20 mins Cook: 25 mins

125g/4oz sunflower spread, refrigerator cold, plus extra for greasing
60g/2oz/⅓ cup caster/superfine sugar, plus extra for dusting
fine zest of 1 lemon
fine zest of 1 orange
180g/6½oz/scant 1½ cups plain/all-purpose flour

1 Preheat the oven to 150°C/300°F/Gas 2 and lightly grease a 20cm/8in shallow cake pan.

2 Put the sunflower spread and sugar in the bowl of a food mixer and beat until the texture is creamy. Mix the lemon and orange zest with the flour, then add this to the creamed mixture and beat until everything is incorporated.

3 Scrape the dough into the prepared pan and spread it out to fill, using your hands. Smooth the top with the back of a spoon. Slice the shortbread into 12 fingers, not going all the way through, and make 2–3 indentations in each slice using the rounded end of a skewer. Bake for 20–25 minutes until it is barely coloured – don't let it overcook. Leave the shortbread to cool in the pan, then sprinkle with a little caster/superfine sugar to serve.

Sour cherry, ginger & almond cookies

These are best eaten on the day of baking. They have a crunch on the outside and a chewy middle, which is just how I like them. If you can't find dried sour cherries, swap to dried blueberries. The spike of ginger is fairly subtle so if you want more, add a generous pinch of ground ginger to the flour.

Makes 16
Prep: 20 mins Cook: 15 mins

150g/5oz/²⁄₃ cup dairy-free spread
150g/5oz/scant 1 cup light soft
    brown sugar
200g/7oz/1²⁄₃ cups self-raising/
    self-rising flour, sifted, plus extra
    for dusting
1 tsp bicarbonate of soda/baking
    soda
40g/1½oz/⅓ cup ground almonds
50g/2oz/²⁄₃ cup flaked/slivered
    almonds
80g/3½oz/²⁄₃ cup dried sour cherries
    or dried blueberries
3 balls of stem ginger, finely
    chopped, plus 1–2 tbsp juice

1 Preheat the oven to 160°C/325°F/Gas 3 and line two baking/cookie sheets with parchment paper.

2 Put the dairy-free spread in the bowl of a food mixer, add the sugar and beat until creamy. In another bowl, mix the flour, bicarbonate of soda/baking soda, ground almonds, flaked/slivered almonds, sour cherries and stem ginger. Add this to the mixer bowl and mix until the ingredients start to come together. Trickle in the ginger juice until it forms a dough. You may not need it all. Tip the mixture onto a floured board and knead gently to a smooth dough. The mixture will be fairly wet, but so as long as it all comes together it will be okay. Don't wrestle with it trying to get it to a firm dough.

3 With floured hands, break up into 16 even-sized balls and sit them on the prepared baking/cookie sheets. Leave plenty of room as they will spread. Flatten each one a little to form a round, wetting your hands, if necessary, and using the heel of your hand to flatten each one so you get a good round-shaped cookie. Bake for 12–15 minutes until golden. They will still be soft but will firm up as they cool. Transfer them to a wire tray to cool, then put the kettle on for your coffee and prepare to tuck in!

Chocolate chip, nutmeg & macadamia cookies

Cookies without eggs do have a different texture, but they still taste pretty good and these are super-easy. The dough is quite wet so let it firm up in the refrigerator for a few hours or overnight – I like to make the dough one day and bake it the next. A pinch of nutmeg adds a warming note. You could also try them with pecans, pistachios or even pine nuts.

Makes about 20
Prep: 20 mins Cook: 20 mins

150g/5oz/⅔ cup sunflower spread
100g/3½oz/½ cup golden caster/
    superfine sugar
100g/3½oz/heaped ½ cup light soft
    brown sugar
1 tsp vanilla extract
225g/8oz/heaped 1¾ cups plain/
    all-purpose flour, sifted
1 tsp bicarbonate of soda/baking
    soda, sifted
a pinch of sea salt
a pinch of freshly grated nutmeg
2 x 100g/3½oz bars of dairy-free
    dark chocolate, at least 70%
    cocoa, roughly broken
50g/1¾oz/½ cup macadamia nuts,
    roughly chopped

1 Put the sunflower spread and both sugars in the bowl of a food mixer and beat until creamy and fluffy. Trickle in the vanilla extract and beat gently, then tip in the flour, bicarbonate of soda/baking soda, salt and nutmeg and beat until well combined. Stir in the chocolate pieces and macadamia nuts, cover the bowl with cling film/plastic wrap and put in the refrigerator to chill for a couple of hours or overnight.

2 When ready to bake, preheat the oven 160°C/325°F/Gas 3 and line two baking/cookie sheets with parchment paper.

3 Scoop out about 20 balls and put them on the prepared baking/cookie sheets, leaving plenty of space for spreading. Press each ball down lightly with the ball of your hand to make a flat round. Bake for 12–15 minutes. They should still be slightly squidgy; they will firm up as they cool. Enjoy while still warm.

Caramelized apple tarte tatin

This upside down tart looks trickier than it is and is equally delicious as an indulgent mid-afternoon treat or a sophisticated dessert. It is super-rich and contains quite a lot of sugar that turns into a delicious toffee sauce, but I think the apples provide a 'healthy' get-out clause if you need one! This is so good served hot with a scoop of vegan ice cream.

Serves 4–6
Prep: 30 mins Cook: 45 mins

200g/7oz/1¼ cup soft brown sugar
1 tbsp sunflower spread
5 eating/dessert apples, peeled, cored and quartered

FOR THE PASTRY
175g/6oz/scant 1½ cups plain/all-purpose flour, plus extra for dusting
zest of 1 lemon
75g/3oz/⅓ cup sunflower spread, refrigerator cold

1 Preheat the oven to 200°C/400°F/Gas 6 and grease a 24cm/9½in cake pan.

2 First make the pastry. Put the flour and lemon zest in a large bowl, add the sunflower spread and rub it all in using your fingertips. Now add a sprinkle of ice cold water – you need very little – and begin to bring the pastry together to form a dough. It should all come away from the sides of the bowl, leaving you with a clean bowl. Roll the dough into a ball and flatten, then cover with cling film/plastic wrap and put in the refrigerator to chill while you cook the toffee and apples.

3 Put the sugar and 3–4 tablespoons of water in a pan and bring almost to the boil, then cook at a high simmer, stirring occasionally, for a few minutes until fudgy. Remove from the heat and pour the sauce into the base of the prepared cake pan. Carefully arrange the apples to fill the pan, being careful not to burn your fingers!

4 Remove the pastry from the refrigerator and roll out on a lightly floured surface. Cut out a round slightly larger than the pan. Place this on top of the apples, tucking in the edges of the pastry. Bake for 30–35 minutes until the pastry is cooked and golden. Remove the tarte tatin from the oven and leave it to cool down slightly for a few minutes, then carefully invert it onto a large plate. Be careful not to spill any of the sauce as there will be quite a lot. Slice the tarte tatin and serve hot or at room temperature.

Fruit & nut chocolate dough ring

It requires some effort to bake bread, but the gain is high. This is a fairly wet dough to start with but do try to resist adding too much more flour as you knead it. The wetter the better! The filling mixture is very adaptable – any favourite fruit and nut mixture goes well, but the chocolate must stay! You could also swap the orange juice for a tipple of vegan sherry.

Serves 14–16
Prep: 20 mins, plus rising
Cook: 30 mins

250ml/9fl oz/generous 1 cup almond milk (you may not need it all)
50g/1¾oz/¼ cup sunflower spread, plus extra for greasing
450g/1lb/3½ cups white strong/bread flour, plus extra for dusting
7g/¼oz/1 sachet fast-action/instant active dried yeast
50g/1¾oz/¼ cup caster/superfine sugar
1 tsp sea salt
icing/confectioners' sugar, sifted, for dusting

FOR THE FILLING
100g/3½oz dairy-free dark chocolate, at least 70% cocoa, broken into squares
150g/5oz/1 cup dried figs or prunes, finely chopped
juice of ½ orange
zest of 1 lemon
40g/1½oz/½ cup flaked/slivered almonds, toasted
40g/1½oz/¼ cup pistachio nuts, chopped
a pinch of freshly grated nutmeg

1 First make the dough. Heat the milk until warm but don't let it boil. Add the sunflower spread and stir until it melts. Add the flour, yeast, sugar and salt to the bowl of a food mixer and mix, using the dough hook, then slowly pour in the warm milk until it becomes a dough. You may not need to add all the milk. Turn the dough out onto a floured board and knead for about 10 minutes until soft, then put it in a large bowl, cover with a damp dish towel and leave somewhere warm for a couple of hours, or until it doubles in size.

2 To make the filling, add the chocolate to a large, heatproof bowl, sit it over a pan of simmering water and stir occasionally until melted. Remove from the heat, add the rest of the ingredients and stir until combined.

3 Knock the air out of the dough and knead for a few minutes, then roll it out to a rectangle, about 42 x 30cm/16 x 12in. Spoon the filling mixture along the long edge, then roll it up into a tube shape. Transfer it to a large, greased baking/cookie sheet and pull the dough round so it meets to make a circle. Sit a large round cutter in the middle. Now make slashes all the way round, about 3cm/1¼in apart. Cover the dough again and leave for another hour, or until it rises again and doubles in size.

4 Preheat the oven to 200°C/400°F/Gas 6.

5 Bake the loaf for 25–30 minutes until golden brown and it sounds hollow when you tap the base. Leave to cool for 10 minutes, then dust with icing/confectioners' sugar. Slice or tear apart to serve.

Sour cherry & pistachio refrigerator cake

A simple no-cook chocolate recipe, this is so easy to make and so good to have in to nibble on or take to friends. I can't resist putting pistachio nuts in because they look so good when it is sliced, and sour cherries work well with dark chocolate. If you can't find dried sour cherries use dried blueberries or mixed cherries and berries.

Serves 14–16
Prep: 20 mins, plus setting

200g/7oz/1⅔ cups dried sour
    cherries
100g/3½oz/¾ cup dried dates or
    figs, roughly chopped
100ml/3½fl oz/scant ½ cup cherry
    brandy or fresh orange or
    cranberry juice
400g/14oz dairy-free dark
    chocolate, at least 70% cocoa,
    broken into squares
125g/4½oz/½ cup sunflower
    spread, plus extra for greasing
2 tbsp golden/light corn syrup
200g/7oz digestive biscuits/Graham
    crackers, broken
100g/3½oz/⅔ cup pistachio nuts,
    chopped
cocoa/unsweetened chocolate
    powder, at least 70% cocoa,
    for dusting

1 Lightly grease and line a 32 x 21cm/12½ x 8½in shallow pan with overhanging parchment paper.

2 Put the cherries and dates in a bowl and pour over the cherry brandy or juice. Leave to one side to let them soften and plump up.

3 Put the chocolate, sunflower spread and golden/light corn syrup in a bowl resting over a pan of just simmering water and stir until melted.

4 Put the biscuits/Graham crackers, nuts and fruit in a large bowl with the juices and stir together, then add the melted chocolate mixture and stir really well until combined and everything is coated. Spoon into the prepared tin, level the top and put it in the refrigerator to chill for a few hours or overnight until firm and hard. Remove and dust liberally with the cocoa and slice to serve.

Banana & walnut loaf cake

The chocolate in this was a last-minute decision, not essential but quite delicious. Leave it out if you prefer. You should get just enough juice from one can of chickpeas/garbanzos for this, but don't worry if it is a little under. The bananas keep this cake moist and sweet but it would be extra delicious drizzled with melted dark chocolate. Pictured on page 218.

Serves 10–12
Prep: 20 mins Cook: 1¼ hours

125g/4oz/½ cup sunflower spread
100ml/3½fl oz/scant ½ cup maple syrup
3 bananas, mashed, plus 1 sliced lengthways
6 tbsp aquafaba (juice from canned chickpeas/garbanzos, see page 16)
125g/4oz/1 cup wholemeal spelt flour, sifted
125g/4oz/1 cup plain/all-purpose flour, sifted
2 tsp baking powder, sifted
a pinch of salt
a pinch of freshly grated nutmeg
100g/3½oz/½ cup golden caster/ superfine sugar
100g/3½oz/1 cup walnuts, chopped
50g/2oz dairy-free dark chocolate, at least 70% cocoa, broken into chunks
100% cocoa/unsweetened chocolate powder, for dusting

1 Preheat the oven to 160°C/325°F/Gas 3 and grease and line a 26 x 7cm/10½ x 2¾in loaf pan with parchment paper.

2 Put the sunflower spread in a pan and heat gently until melted, then stir in the maple syrup and mashed banana and the aquafaba. Heat it all gently and mix together until combined. Leave to one side.

3 Put the flours, baking powder, salt, nutmeg and sugar in a bowl and mix together, then pour in the wet mixture and beat together using a wooden spoon until smooth. Stir in the walnuts and chocolate pieces. Spoon the mixture into the prepared pan and level the top, then top with the sliced banana, pushing it slightly into the mixture. Bake for 1–1¼ hours, or until a skewer comes out clean when poked in the middle.

4 Put it on a wire rack and leave to cool for about 15 minutes in the pan, then turn it out onto the wire rack and let it cool completely before dusting with a little cocoa/unsweetened chocolate powder. Slice and serve!

Chocolate & espresso 'salami' with prunes

I've put two favourite flavours in here that I like with chocolate: coffee and prunes. I love making this as it doesn't involve the cooker and when it comes to baking I am a lazy cook. It is rather rich so slice it as finely as you can to nibble on and, yes, it is good with a cup of coffee! As this is an Italian dish, I like to use amaretti biscotti, and the brand Orgran are gluten-free and vegan. You could use digestives/Graham crackers if that's easier, as many supermarket brands just happen to be vegan.

Makes about 30 slices
Prep: 20 mins, plus chilling
Cook: 5 mins

200g/7oz dairy-free dark chocolate, at least 70% cocoa
100g/3½oz/scant ½ cup sunflower spread
200g/7oz amaretti biscotti, coarsely chopped
2 tbsp espresso coffee
50g/2oz/scant ½ cup ready-to-eat prunes, chopped
200g/7oz/1⅔ cups mixed nuts, such as almonds, skin on, pistachios and hazelnuts
icing/confectioners' sugar, sifted, for dusting

1 Put the chocolate in an ovenproof bowl, sit it over a pan of barely simmering water and heat gently until it melts, then let it cool slightly.

2 Put the sunflower spread in the bowl of a food mixer and beat until creamy. Add the biscuits, espresso, prunes, nuts and melted chocolate and beat on slow to combine.

3 Spoon the mixture out onto a large sheet of parchment paper, roll the paper up into a sausage shape and secure the ends with a twist. You can also wrap it in cling film/plastic wrap and tightly roll it. Put it in the refrigerator to set for at least 4 hours or overnight.

4 When you are ready to serve, unroll the salami, and dust with icing/confectioners' sugar to coat. Tie up with string to complete the 'salami' effect, if you wish.

Blueberry & lemon muffins

A recipe for vegan muffins is great to have in your repertoire as they are incredibly easy to make and you can vary the flavour and fruit to suit. They are also very forgiving as they don't require beating like a sponge cake. In fact, quite the opposite: lumpy batter is good. They are best eaten on the day of baking so are good to make when friends are coming over. I've used a mix of flours as I think spelt flour adds a delicious hint of nuttiness. Drizzle with a little icing/confectioners' sugar for extra sweetness.

Makes 12
Prep: 20 mins Cook: 25 mins

2 tbsp chia seeds
250g/9oz/2 cups spelt flour, sifted
125g/4oz/1 cup plain/all-purpose
    flour, sifted
1 tsp baking powder, sifted
1 tsp bicarbonate of soda/baking
    soda, sifted
1 tsp ground cinnamon
zest and juice of 1 lemon
a pinch of salt
125g/4oz/⅔ cup light soft
    brown sugar
250ml/9fl oz/generous 1 cup
    almond milk
100ml/3½fl oz/scant ½ cup
    rapeseed oil or sunflower oil
2 tsp vanilla extract
300g/10½oz/2½ cups fresh
    blueberries or blackberries if in
    season
icing/confectioners' sugar, for dusting

1 Preheat the oven to 200°C/400°F/Gas 6 and line a 12-hole muffin pan with paper muffin cases/liners.

2 Mix the chia seeds with 6 tablespoons of water and leave to one side for 10 minutes or so, then mix.

3 Put the flours, baking powder, bicarbonate of soda/baking soda, cinnamon, lemon zest and salt in a bowl and mix really well together, then stir in the sugar.

4 In another bowl, mix the milk, lemon juice, oil and vanilla together, then stir in the chia seed mixture. Add this to the flour mixture, then stir in the blueberries or blackberries and beat briefly with a wooden spoon to a rough batter. Divide the mixture up evenly among the muffin cases/liners.

5 Bake for about 25 minutes, or until risen and pale golden. Leave to cool slightly, then dust with icing/confectioners' sugar to serve. These are best eaten on the day of baking and even better eaten whilst still warm.

Raw brownies with chocolate yogurt topping

These are altogether different from the baked brownies that you may be used to, but despite being 'raw' these retain the unctuous chocolate squidge of a traditional brownie and will sit happily in your fridge ready to sate any chocolate cravings. Pictured overleaf.

Makes 12 large squares
Prep 20 mins, plus setting
Cook: 5 mins

125g/4oz/¾ cup dried figs
75g/3oz/½ cup ready-to-eat dates, pitted
75g/3oz/½ cup ready-to-eat prunes, pitted
75g/3oz/½ cup cashew nuts
75g/3oz/½ cup flaked/slivered almonds
75g/3oz/½ cup hazelnuts
75g/3oz/½ cup pecan nuts
5 tbsp cocoa/unsweetened chocolate powder, at least 70% cocoa
1 tbsp maple syrup

FOR THE FROSTING
200g/7oz dairy-free dark chocolate, at least 70% cocoa, broken into small even pieces
½ avocado, pitted and mashed
4–5 tbsp soy yogurt
1 tbsp maple syrup

1 Line a 21 x 30cm/8½ x 12in shallow pan with overhanging parchment paper. Put the dried fruit in a bowl and pour in enough boiling water so it just covers. Leave the fruit to soak and plump up a little.

2 Put the nuts in the bowl of a food processor and whiz until roughly chopped. Then tip in the fruit and the soaking water and whiz until blended but still with some texture – it is best to use the pulse button. Add the cocoa/unsweetened chocolate powder and maple syrup and pulse to combine. Scrape the mixture out into the prepared pan, spread it out and smooth the top. Put in the refrigerator to chill and set for a few hours.

3 Meanwhile, make the frosting. Put the chocolate in a heatproof bowl and sit it over a pan of simmering water. Stir until melted, remove from the heat and let it cool slightly.

4 Put the avocado, most of the yogurt, the maple syrup and cooled chocolate in the bowl of a food mixer and beat until smooth, adding more yogurt if needed.

5 Spread the mixture over the fruit and nut base, mark out squares and put it in the refrigerator for a few hours or overnight to chill and set. Slice to serve. This will happily keep in the refrigerator for a week.

Carrot cake with maple syrup frosting

This cake can be as humble or extravagant as you want – leave it naked and enjoy a slice with an afternoon cup of tea or slather it with fondant and it's fit for a celebration. The chia seeds aren't just for crunch, they act as a binding agent in place of eggs. Carrots make this cake lovely and moist and the mix of spices brings a fragrant warmth. Pictured overleaf.

Serves 10–12
Prep: 30 mins Cook: 35 mins

3 tbsp chia seeds
125g/4oz/1 cup wholemeal spelt
    flour, sifted
125g/4oz/1 cup plain/all-purpose
    flour, sifted
2 tsp baking powder, sifted
½ tsp bicarbonate of soda/baking
    soda, sifted
1 tsp ground ginger
a generous pinch of freshly grated
    nutmeg
1 tsp ground cinnamon
zest and juice of 1 orange
200g/7oz/1¼ cups soft light
    brown sugar
300ml/10½fl oz/1¼ cups sunflower
    oil
300g/10½oz/2½ cups grated carrots
    (about 5–6 carrots)
100g/3½oz/1 cup pecan nuts,
    chopped
100g/3½oz/¾ cup sultanas/golden
    raisins

FOR THE FROSTING
125g/4oz/½ cup sunflower spread
500g/1lb 2oz/3½ cups icing/
    confectioners' sugar, sifted
3 tbsp maple syrup

1 Preheat the oven to 180°C/350°F/Gas 4 and line two 20cm/8in loose-bottomed springform cake pans with parchment paper.

2 Mix the chia seeds with 9 tablespoons of cold water and leave to one side for about 10 minutes so they soak up the water, then mix.

3 Put the flours, baking powder, bicarbonate of soda/baking soda, spices, orange zest and sugar in a large bowl and mix to combine. In another bowl, put the orange juice, oil and chia seed mixture and stir to combine. Add this to the flour mixture and stir well, then add the carrots, three-quarters of the nuts and the sultanas/golden raisins and stir again.

4 Divide the mixture equally between the pans, level the tops and bake for 30–35 minutes until risen and golden and a skewer comes out clean from the middle. If it has wet mixture on it, leave it for another 5 minutes, then test again. When ready, remove the pans from the oven and leave to cool on a wire rack for 10 minutes, then loosen the edges, turn the cakes out onto the wire rack and leave to cool completely.

5 To make the frosting, put the sunflower spread in the bowl of a food mixer and beat until creamy, then slowly add half the icing/confectioners' sugar, then the maple syrup, then keep adding the icing/confectioners' sugar until it is the right consistency – not too stiff but not at all runny.

6 Spread half the frosting over one of the cakes then sandwich them together. Top the cake with remaining frosting, then scatter with the remaining nuts. Leave until the topping has set, then slice to serve.